World-Famous

Strange Mysteries

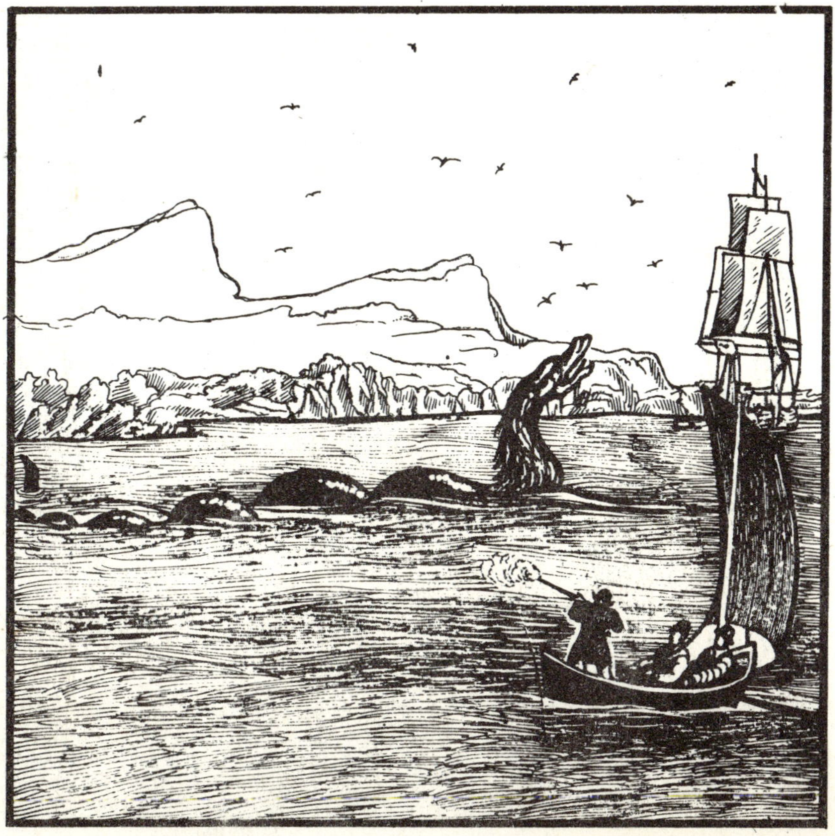

World-Famous Strange Mysteries

Author
Mrs. Geeta Lal Sahai

Editor
Dr. J.G. Varma

PUSTAK MAHAL®

Administrative office and sale centre
J-3/16 , Daryaganj, New Delhi-110002
☎ 23276539, 23272783, 23272784 • *Fax:* 011-23260518
E-mail: info@pustakmahal.com • *Website:* www.pustakmahal.com

Branches
Bengaluru: ☎ 080-22234025 • *Telefax:* 080-22240209
E-mail: pustakmahalblr@gmail.com
Mumbai: ☎ 022-22010941, 022-22053387
E-mail: rapidex@bom5.vsnl.net.in
Patna: ☎ 0612-3294193 • *Telefax:* 0612-2302719
E-mail: rapidexptn@rediffmail.com

ISBN 978-81-223-0558-6

Edition: 2015

Printed at : Radha Offset, Delhi

Preface

It is the second book in 'World-Famous Series' on Mysteries. The success of the first book has inspired us to bring out the second book.

Our primary motive is to present to the readers some of the "Strange Mysteries" in a simple and attractive manner. The reader will judge for himself the unresolved and mysterious phenomena and will try to answer the queries which arise in human mind.

We have also tried to include some of the scientific mysteries as well which are concerned with psychology, parapsychology, psychiatry and the life sciences.

Thus we have covered a vast field and have picked up the very important and salient mysteries of the world. The treatment is no doubt authoritative, and the facts which are presented are genuine. The selected photographs add to the value of the book.

We are confident that the book will win the appreciation of the readers and will be a source of joy to them.

—Publishers

Contents

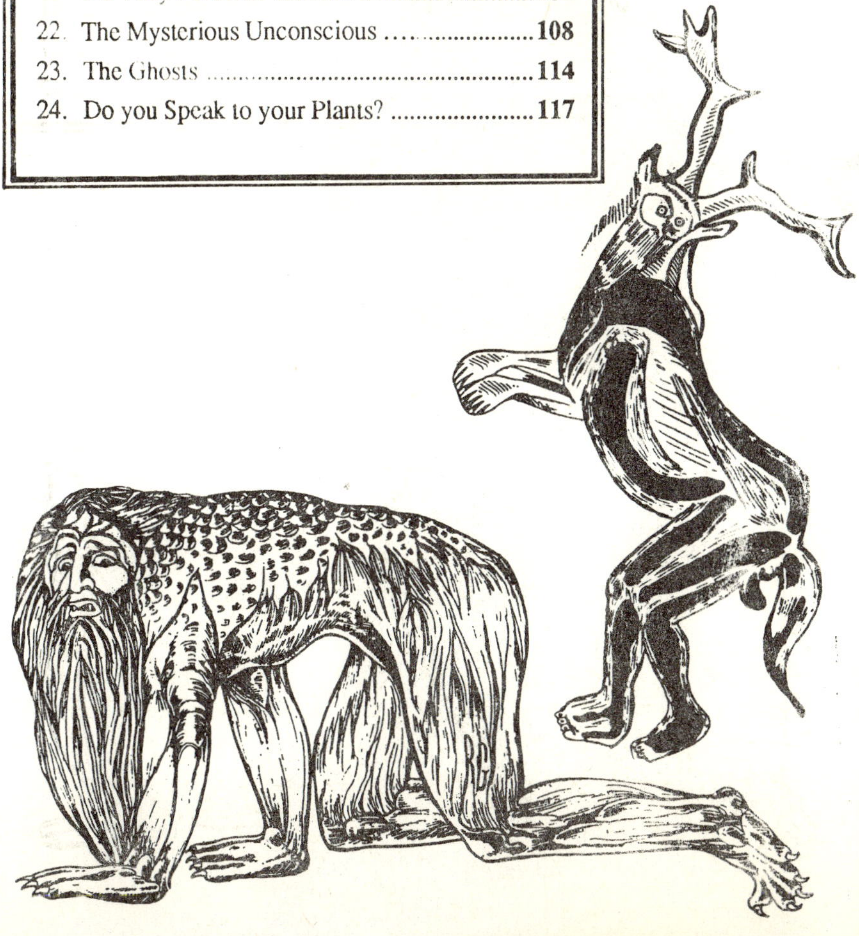

Why Are Visitors Dying ?

The search for Tutankhamun's tomb continued for several years before the excavators finally discovered it. But, surprisingly enough, after its excavation, several persons involved in it either fell ill or passed away. Lord Carnarvon, who discovered the tomb, was the first unfortunate person to die suddenly. After him a trail of victims followed. Naturally the question arises: why did people die after visiting Tutankhamun's tomb?

The tomb of Tutankhamun was discovered after a long search. Many archaeologists had earlier failed to locate it. Earl Carnarvon along with Harold Carter discovered Tutankhamun's tomb on November 26, 1922 after a long time. With its discovery, the complexion of the area changed. The tourists flocked in large numbers to have its glimpse.

The innermost of the three coffins which contained the mummy of Tutankhamun. It was made of pure gold.

However, Carnarvon and Carter had to close down the tomb because of the very great stress of work. Further, their relations deteriorated as they entered into a dispute over the ownership of the articles found in the tomb. Being very much dejected, Carnarvon returned to England. And then happened the unexpected. Carnarvon fell sick. He suffered from intermittent fever. He moved to Cairo. His wife, daughter and son also accompanied him. Carter was also informed of his poor health and he immediately joined the unhappy family. But Carnarvon sunk into a coma and died in the early hours of April 5. He was just fifty seven. At the time of his death, the entire Cairo city was plunged into

Lord Carnarvon standing at the place chosen by him for his burial on the summit of Beacon Hill.

The body of the Pharaoh preserved in a gold coffin and placed in a sarcophagus still lies in its chamber.

darkness. Nobody could explain the reason for that complete blackout. More astonishing was the fact that in England, Carnarvon's fox-terrier, Susan, suddenly began to howl and passed away.

Thus started the great journey of Tutankhamun's 'curse' which took Carnarvon's life within two months of the discovery of the tomb. Everybody was shocked for one could realize the veracity of hieroglyphics carved on the entrance of the tomb: 'Death shall come to him who touches the tomb.'

Very few persons believed in the truth of the hieroglyphics, but fewer still disbelieved it. Lord Carnarvon's son also said that he neither believed nor disbelieved the veracity of the written characters. According to him, soon after the death of his father, he was visited by an unknown woman who told him not to visit his father's grave. He obeyed her orders and did not go near his father's grave.

Besides Lord Carnarvon, a few other archaeologists and tourists who visited the tomb were either taken ill or died in peculiar circumstances. The disbelievers in the 'curse' say that these people must have been ill beforehand or probably their death was due to the strains of travel and effects of dust, heat and excitement.

Professor La Flour paid a visit to the tomb on his first day in Luxor and died that very night in the room of the hotel where he was staying. An American millionaire died after developing fever on the very day that he visited the tomb. Carter's assistants, Mace and Bethell, also suffered from fever frequently and finally died.

Some researchers tried to explain the mysterious phenomena by suggesting that the fungus covering the walls of the tomb would have triggered off allergy or infection. It was also suggested that the ancient Egyptians had used their knowledge of poisons to protect the secrets of their King.

As the researchers were busy trying to disprove the theory of curse, more persons became its victims. Dr. Gamel ed-Din Mehrez, Director of the Department of Antiquities, took Tutankhamun's relics to America. He did not believe in the theory of 'curse'. He said, "All my life I've been involved with tombs and mummies. I am surely the best proof that it is all coincidence." A few weeks later, he died most unexpectedly at the age of fifty two.

In 1980, the British television team began the production of a film entitled, "The Curse of King Tut." On the very first day of shooting something terrible happened. The hero of the film fractured his leg at ten places, when a vintage car, which was being used, jumped over the edge

The young king being anointed by his Queen. Howard Carter said, "It is the most beautiful thing that has been found in Egypt."

of a hill. His role was taken up by another actor, but other members of the team refused to cooperate.

Strange coincidences have refused to let the 'curse' legend die. Whether these deaths were mere coincidences or not is debatable. But in the absence of any sound reason for the mysterious deaths occurring every time after a visit to Tutankhamun's tomb, has made some people say that it would have been much better if the tomb would have been left untouched. Perhaps they are correct!

Miraculous Cars and Castles

What is the connection between a curse and the victim's clothes, house, car, pen etc.? "Obviously nothing", a scientific mind may claim. Yet there are many records of houses, cars, castles,particular type and colour of clothes that seem to have brought unimaginable disaster to their owners. What exactly is the connection between them? However, a connection does seem to exist, so much so that according to some, a 'cursed' car was responsible for the World War I and subsequent deaths of its owners.

The world of unnatural happenings is really unbelievable. Luck or ill-luck seems to be embedded in certain objects: clothes, cars, houses, pens, art-pieces, etc. There is no scientific theory about them, yet the bizarre incidents have been reported throughout the world and are found associated with them.

The car that brought ill-luck to the world. Archduke Ferdinand and his wife were killed in this car.

General Potiorek, who purchased the car of the Archduke Ferdinand, invited bad luck on himself.

A well known case of ill-luck is associated with the car of the Archduke Francis Ferdinand. He was heir to the throne of Austria and Hungary. He and his wife were travelling in a car when they were assassinated in it in 1914. The murder proved to be too costly. It gave birth to the World War 1. Nobody cursed the car at that time.

Later it was bought by General Potiorek of the Austrian army. But apparently the car had the magical powers of bringing ill-luck to its owner. A few weeks later, this brave General suffered a crushing defeat at Valjevo. He could not bear the shock and disgrace and lost his mental equilibrium. He died as an insane man.

However, the journey of the car was not yet complete. An Austrian captain bought it. And within a fortnight, the boulder of ill-luck fell on him. He first killed two peasants, lost control of the car, bumped against a tree and subsequently fractured his neck.

After the War, the car was bought by the Governor of Yugoslavia. As long as the car stayed with him, a trail of accidents took place. In just four months, four fatal accidents occurred. The Governor also lost his hand in an accident. He became superstitious and sold the car to a doctor. The doctor could enjoy the luxury of the car just for six months. Later he was crushed to death inside it. The next victim was a wealthy jeweller, who committed suicide. The next owner-victim was a Swiss racing driver. He was killed in a race when the car threw him over a wall. The next unfortunate owner was a Siberian farmer. The car's last owner was a garage owner Tibor Hirshfeld who, along with his four friends, was killed in an accident.

After such a long list of unfortunate incidents, the car's fate was sealed. It was taken to the Vienna museum. Since then it is there and no untoward incident has happened in the museum.

Somewhat similar is the story of a statuette of a half-naked fat man. This idol was the Japanese god of 'Good Luck'. It was at display in a junk shop, when a middle-aged English couple, Mr and Mrs C.J. Lambert, saw it and bought it at a very low price.

With the possession of this statue, a long trail of ill-luck visited them. Ironically 'Good Luck' became 'ill luck' for them. Both of them

Ho-tei, the Japanese god of Good Luck

suffered from various ailments. They kept on suffering from one disease or the other till the god of 'good luck' stayed with them. Finally some good sense prevailed on over them and they could sell it to a Japanese manager of an oriental art shop. The couple never entered that shop again.

Such cases abound. One wonders at their queerness and ask: what exactly is the connection between an object and its owner? Psychologists and analysts explain that there is something in the attitudes of such people. Such people, researchers explain, develop a negative attitude and have a feeling that 'something bad' is going to happen. Hence, it has been suggested that possibly the accidents occur due to the prejudices existing in the victim's unconscious mind.

Not all agree with the above theory. The journalist and the psychic investigator, Edward Russel, has put forward the theory that there may be some connection between 'the negative thought field' and the 'curse' that seems to afflict the people. According to his theory, the thought fields implant themselves in objects like an electric field which produces patterns on magnetic recording tape.

This argument is more reasonable than the previous one, but it is not wholly satisfactory. The sceptics do not completely agree with this theory. They question the connection of houses, castles, ships and airplanes with the misfortunes of their occupants.

Gerard Croiset, a Dutch psychometrist, advanced the theory that inanimate objects transfer strong physical and atmospheric impressions. A psychometrist can know many things about an object merely by holding it in his hands. He has the capacity to feel and read the impressions given out by an object. It is true that sometimes souls, continue to dwell in the most precious object of the deceased.

The following story is not dated centuries back. In 1938 Eikichi Suzeki deposited the precious doll of his sister, Kiku, in a temple in the village of Monji Saiwai Cho in Japan. The doll was the most treasured item of his dead sister. Since he was going to the War, he carefully put the doll into a box with his sister's ashes.

Suzuki returned from the War in 1947. He immediately went to the temple and opened the box in front of the priest. To their surprise, they discovered that the doll's hair had grown in length. The doll was scientifically examined and every thing was found to be intact. It was human hair that had grown. The doll was then placed on the altar, but its

The doll of Kiku

hair continued to grow. In fact it is still growing and the altar has become a place of pilgrimage. Nobody has been able to comprehend its reason. In all probability the soul of the little girl resides in the doll, the object which was dearest to her.

No doubt such unfathomable and unique cases baffle the common man. They motivate scientists to perform long and arduous experiments in search of the truth. But their efforts have not been successful so far in this direction. ■

The Mysterious Men in Black

The Men in Black invite a great deal of attention. As UFO sightings increase, so does the harassment of the witnesses by some mysterious men, who are always dressed in black.
Many people had an encounter with them. But nobody was able to furnish their exact description. After all, who are these peculiar and mystifying men in black?

Albert Bender, Director of the International Flying Saucer Bureau based in Connecticut, USA, was to publish his momentous findings in his journal, 'Space Review'. But he could not do so. The three Men in Black prevented him from passing on his discovery. Bender said, "They looked like clergymen, but wore hats similar to (the style of) Homburg. Their faces were not clearly discernible, for the hats partly hid and shaded them..........."

Bender was so much terrified by them that he closed down his organisation and even ceased publication of his journal.

Albert Bender, American UFO investigator

In September 1976, Dr Herbert Hopkins was acting as a consultant on an alleged UFO teleportation case in Maine, USA. One fine evening, when his wife and children were away, he received a telephone call from a man, who identified himself as one from New Jersey UFO Research Organisation. The man wanted to meet Dr Hopkins and the latter agreed. Dr Hopkins went to the back door to switch on the lights, so that his visitor could find the way easily. But when he went there, he was surprised to see a man already climbing up the stairs. However, Dr Hopkins welcomed his visitor.

The visitor discussed the UFO case with Dr Hopkins. After a while, he gave two coins to Dr. Hopkins and told him to put one coin in his hand. Dr Hopkins did so. Then the visitor asked the Doctor to watch the coin. Dr Hopkins did as he was asked to do. He noticed the coin slowly moving out of focus and then disappearing completely. The visitor sarcastically remarked, "Nobody will ever see that coin again." After a little while, the mysterious man got up and said, "My energy is running low. I must go now. Good Bye." Dr Hopkins saw him descending the stairs. When he was leaving, Dr. Hopkins also saw a bright light shining in the driveway, a bluish white and distinctly brighter than a normal car lamp.

Men in Black

When Dr Hopkins family returned, they found marks in the centre of the driveway. They were astonished as these marks could not have been made by a car. More astonishing was the fact that next day no marks were visible.

Dr Hopkins was so much scared that he erased all tapes of hypnotic sessions. His son also narrated some bizarre incidents which were occurring at his place. But more shocking was the realisation that the place mentioned by the visitor, New Jersey UFO Research Organisation, never existed.

However, the UFO researchers and investigators are not the only people to receive such visitors. Dr Hopkins has given us an account which is most exhaustive. One cannot overlook these incidents or pass them over as mere figments of imagination. For why should a respectable person like Dr Hopkins resort to such a narration of a tale. His incident cannot be dismissed as a delusion because other members of the family saw the marks of the car and also reported a series of disturbances on the telephone that seemed to commence immediately after the visit of the Man in the Black. Hence, after cross-checking every minute detail, the experts arrived at the conclusion that such an incident must have happened, although their nature remains mysterious till this day.

The Men in Black incidents usually happen after a UFO sighting. The person, who has seen it or an investigator on the case receives a visitor. The victim is usually alone at the time of the visit at his own home. The visitors are generally three in number and arrive in a black car. The registration number of the car is invariably a nonexistent one. The most peculiar thing is that the visitors are mostly men. Rarely is there a woman amongst them. If a woman is there, it is never more than one. In appearance, these men resemble the stereotyped image of a CIA agent or a Secret Service man. Their dress is dark from head to foot: their hats, suits, ties, shoes and socks are all black. They have a cold expression on their faces and conclude their visits with a note of warning that nothing was to be revealed about UFOs to any one. They suddenly disappear after threatening the subject with violent consequences, in case their visit was ever revealed to others.

Often their instructions were flouted, but nothing drastic happened. No doubt they excel in harassing the witnesses with their untimely visits and telephone calls. Sometimes they just frighten the subjects with their presence.

The question, then, arises: Who actually are these mysterious Men in Black? In 1970, an American theorist, Tony Kimery, linked the mysterious MIB (as Men in Black are often called) to the complex UFO phenomenon. And this, in turn, was a part of another big and complex phenomenon. Kimery wrote, "It is known that projects by them are now under way for the complete control of .... the political, financial, religious and scientific institutions. They, the MIB, have a very long background and history that stretches back to centuries and indicates a massive build-up concentration to the place where it is to-day."

The researchers have repeatedly emphasised that MIB phenomenon originates from some psychic or mental link between the witness and the MIB. They believe that though the witness "braves the threat and continues to tell the world of his experiences, it has been observed that the MIB seems powerless to act against him." The researchers cite the case of Carlos de Los Santos in support of their statement.

Santos was going for the television interview when he was stopped by a gang. He cancelled the interview and immediately went back home. However, a friend later on assured him of all safety and prodded him to give the interview. Santos went ahead with it. And nothing untoward happened to him!

Nonetheless, people do not agree with the theory that MIB threat is just imaginary. According to them, the subject is of a more serious nature and needs further research.

Anyhow, whatever be the exact nature of the MIB, whether they are illusory or real, the entire phenomenon has left an unforgettable impression on the minds of their victims. Besides, the MIB phenomenon is very vital for the sociologists to comprehend. Day by day, the MIB are now being compared to the forgotten past of the unbelievable witch, the vampire and the werewolf. ■

Strange Mysteries of the Past

Past is often like Pandora's box and when the lid is opened it invariably sends out shock waves. The giant glass slab discovered in a cave in Galilee (Israel) puzzled the modern man. The measurements showed that it was the third largest piece of glass ever made. The other two were made in 1934. This piece was 1,000 years old.

So what was it doing in a cave? Who created it at that time and how the incredible feat was achieved?

The other puzzling archaeological mystery is about the Chinese aluminium. It was discovered accidentally by the labourers in a buried tomb. And the mystery amazed archaeologists and scientists for quite some time, as it made historians reconsider historical facts all over again.

The Amazing Glass Slab

With the new archaeological finds, the mysteries of the past are growing more and more complicated. The 20th century man is astonished to know that even during earlier times, man was quite advanced and has left behind such stupendous artefacts and buildings which are, technically speaking, enigmas to this day. And one such enigma is the great glass slab of Galilee.

Local authorities had decided to convert a cave at Beth she'arim into a museum. The cave generated a lot of interest and speculation because it was situated at a site of an ancient city where Jews were mercilessly buried in catacombs. The work soon began in full swing. At the time of excavation, the cave was used as a water tank and was badly silted up. A bulldozer had to be called to clear up the mess. The bulldozer had hardly started cleaning up when suddenly the machine stopped in the middle of the floor. A large slab had struck it. The authorities of the museum liked the slab and preserved it as an item of display.

The cave that was newly turned into a museum was opened to public and surprisingly for years the slab was used as a stand on which the model of the building was exhibited. Visitors came and passed by the slab,

The Great Glass Slab of Galilee

noticing only the model. Thus the slab remained there for years unnotice and neglected.

It was only in 1960 that some archaeologists noticed its peculiarity. They closely examined the slab and to their amazement, they discovered that it was not made of rock but of a peculiar purplish green glass. The discovery attracted experts from all over the world in great numbers. In 1964, a team of American experts under Dr Robert Brill, Administrator of Scientific Research at the Corning Museum of Glass, New York, arrived. The team thoroughly checked the slab and was surprised to know that the slab was made of glass. More surprising were the mathematical calculations. It measured 3.40 by 1.94 metres and was 50 cms thick. It weighed 8.8 tons. These calculations made it the third largest glass slab. The other two were produced in 1934 in America, but this glass slab, according to the archaeologists,was well over 1,000 years old. The experts were curious to know about its history. They wanted to know as to how an ancient man ever succeeded in making a magnificent large glass as this. What was it doing in a cave? And finally who made it?

The answer to the first question was easily found out. Dr Brill, along with the members of his team, excavated beneath the slab. There he discovered many large stones which, according to him, must have been covered with clay where glass was mixed and heated. His guess was

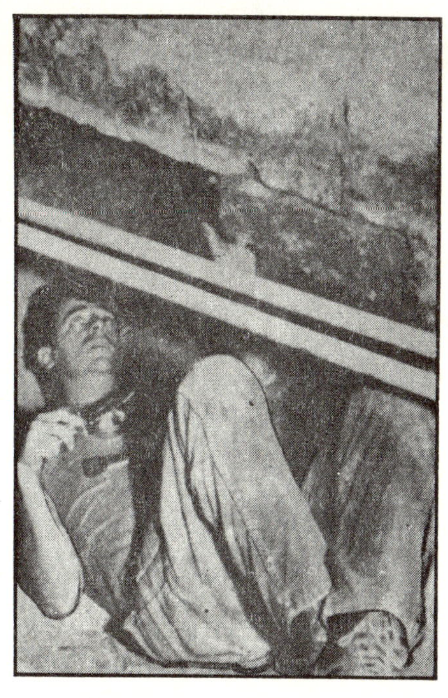

Dr Robert Brill excavating beneath the slab. He established that "it is one of the largest pieces of glass ever known to have been made by man".

confirmed by the archaeologists who said that a layer of large stones was found there sometime ago.

The history of the cave was further analysed. The historical date suggested that the slab was made between the 4th and the early 7th century A.D. It was manufactured to be designed into decorative glass objects or perhaps to be used for beautifying architectural forms.

However, both the suggestions were merely guesses and Dr Brill himself was not satisfied with the above hypothesis. So the purpose behind making of such a giant glass slab of Galilee has remained a mystery till this day. Accepting it as an astonishing piece of superb ancient technology, we are still groping in the dark about its other details. The intentions of the Galilean glass-makers stay buried in the tantalising silence of the past.

Forgotten Tomb

It was the first day of the last month of the year 1952. Labourers were busy making a sports field in the Jiangsu Province. Since the sports field was to be made for the Jingvi Middle School of Vixing city, the land was chosen very cautiously. The chosen piece of land was surrounded by an oblong hillock and had four mounds. It was indeed difficult for labourers to remove the mounds. However, labourers were busy doing their work as usual when suddenly, a labourer shrieked with astonishment for his spade had struck a thin layer. There a hole was visible. Everybody peeped inside. And even in darkness they could see some peculiar objects inside.

The naive labourers were frightened. They quickly called the police. The police went down the small opening and announced to everyone's surprise that a major archaeological discovery had been made. The place was sealed and soon archaeologists thronged the place. The excavation started and it became clear that the place was a tomb, and there were two tombs instead of one. The tombs had been built in a peculiar style. Each tomb had a chamber which had an arched roof and was constructed of wedge shaped bricks. On it there was a square slab. While some bricks covered the floor, the roof was covered with faces of animals.

The task of dating was quite easy. The inscription on one tomb read: "20th September of the seventh year of Yuan Kang the late General Zhou ....." And on the other, the official titles and signatures were inscribed. So archaeologists concluded that it must have been the tomb of a nobleman called Zhou Chu, a great military leader and scholar, who lived during the rule of Jin dynasty from 265 A.D. to 420 A.D. Zhou Chu was a great military man and had died fighting the Tibetans in 297 A.D.

However, these were mere historical facts. But the real discovery which astonished the world related to the pieces of metal found in one of the tombs. In the beginning these were considered to be useless objects. But when they were chemically examined, the results shocked the world. They were pieces of pure aluminium. This was a bewildering fact because aluminium was unknown to the Western world till the beginning of the 19th century. This discovery made the historians consider whether Chinese were more advanced than Europeans and secondly whether Chinese knew the production of electricity, for which aluminium is largely required.

The sceptics did not agree that aluminium was produced in that period. Even Chinese historians also doubted its historical validity. According to some critics it must have been dropped by grave robbers later on. The world was not ready to accept that the Chinese knew the production of aluminium. The researchers from the University of St. Andrews conducted an exhaustive survey in 1980 and concluded that the entire discovery was a 'hoax'. But in 1985 the Chinese geologists claimed that they had found grains of 'native aluminium' in Guizhou province. 'Native aluminium' is a rare commodity and has been found at very few places. The recent Chinese discovery has once again revived the aluminium controversy. It has confirmed the possibility of the fact that aluminium found in the tomb was genuine. ■

Coincidences and Life

What is a coincidence? How and why does it happen? These are some of the questions which we often ask about coincidences. So far nobody has been able to fathom the reasons behind them. Yet almost everyone has experienced the consequences of this phenomenon in his or her life at one stage or the other. And, surprisingly enough, coincidences occur even in most trivial things of life.

A young aspiring actor was to appear before an interview board. It was a golden chance for him to prove his mettle. But the book from which he was to prepare his role was not available to him. He searched for the book everywhere, but could not find it. Ultimately, with great disappointment, he boarded the city bus to return home. In the bus a middle-aged man, who was carrying some books, stood by him. As the bus became over-crowded, he requested the young man to hold some books for him. But when he got down, he just forgot to take back those books.

At first the actor did not know what do to. But eventually, just out of curiosity, he took out the first book and, to his great surprise, he found it to be the drama book 'Tughlak', he was so desperately looking for. Next day, when he appeared before the examining committee, there was another surprise for him. That middle-aged man whom he had met in the bus, was one of the Committee members. The young man returned the book to the owner and thanked him. The member of the Committee was also non-plussed.

On 6 August 1978, Pope Paul VI lay on his deathbed. The little precious alarm clock which he had bought in 1923 was beside him as usual. For the last 55 years the clock had been Pope's most faithful servant. Like an obedient pet, it had awakened him every morning at six O'clock. But on that inauspicious day, it started ringing at 9.40 p.m., the time when Pope lay dead.

This was the most strange case of coincidence. But there are several

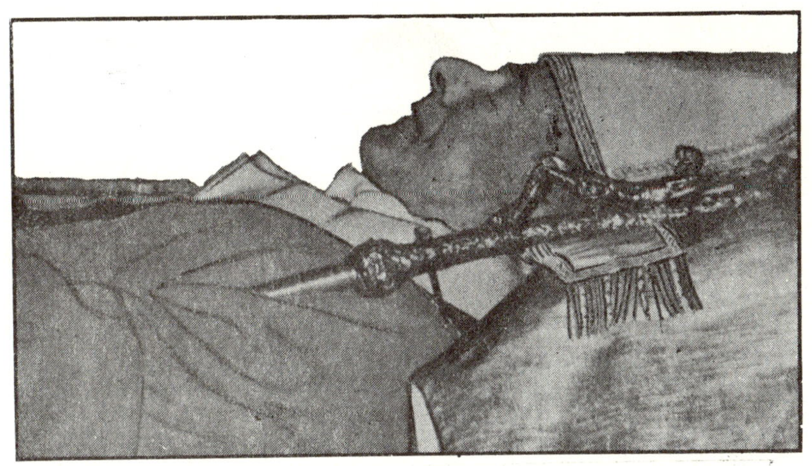

Pope Paul VI lying in state at 9.40 p.m. on 6th August 1978.

other strange cases of coincidence. No wonder they have perplexed scientists, philosophers and mathematicians alike. For more than 2,000 years, they have been trying to unravel the hidden messages of coincidences. They have tried to answer the questions relating to the nature and meanings of coincidences and also to discover the hidden forces lying behind them.

In the 4th century B.C., Hippocrates suggested that the world was linked together and it was one big mass of land not separated by water; coincidences, therefore, were nothing but sympathetic elements seeking each other.

In the 19th century, the famous philosopher, Arthur Schopenhauer, explained that coincidences were nothing but "simultaneous happenings of unconnected events."

Much later in the 20th century, Dr Paul Kammerer scientifically conducted his experiments for days and months by recording people's talks and also noting down the details of their personality inclusive of their age, sex, dress or any other relevant characteristic thereof. Finally Kammerer published his conclusions in the form of a book entitled, "The Law of Seriality". In this book he had come to the conclusion that coincidences came in series and they were a kaleidoscopic exposition of various unknown cosmic forces.

After Kammerer, two European minds combined their efforts.

Wofang Pauli (1900 -1958), the Nobel prize-winning physicist who, together with the eminent psychologist C.G. Jung, introduced the concept of synchronicity to extend Kammerer's theory of seriatity. The acausal principle of synchronicity helped the occurrence of coincidences.

These two men were Wolfgang Pauli and the Swiss psychologist and philosopher Professor Carl Gustav Jung. Both of them exhaustively researched the controversial topic and concluded that coincidences were nothing but "the visible traces of the untraceable principles". A single mysterious force at work in the universe tries to harmonise the disharmonised life. Thus it imposes its own discipline over the confusion and chaos of human life.

More recently, Arthur Koestler, a science journalist, also extensively researched the phenomena of coincidences and explained them as "puns of destiny".

Koestler worked intensively and wrote extensively to search out a scientific basis for the occurrence of coincidences. The phrase 'puns of destiny' was used by him to explain the philosophical implications of coincidences.

Whether a coincidence is a 'pun of destiny' or not cannot be scientifically proved. But the fact is that the entire exercise has an air of mystery about it. It is so very difficult to know what exactly coincidences are, especially when so many peculiar and important incidents do happen together. In fact all explanations touch merely a fringe of this problem. But we cannot reasonably dismiss sudden meaningful incidents as mere coincidences. They have a purpose to fulfil in the cosmic whole, which has to be deciphered. We give below examples of some *meaningful incidents.*

Arthur Koestler

The year was 1944. The world was locked into one of its cruellest wars. Nazis were hated and feared. The entire world was planning to overthrow the Nazis and save the world from annihilation. Every operation was planned in a code word. The various code words were: 'Overlord', 'Neptune', 'Utah', 'Omaha' and 'Mulberry'. The topple was to take place on June 6. Strangely enough, all these words appeared in a crossword puzzle of 'Daily Telegraph', exactly 33 days before this important date. The secret service men immediately swung into action. They arrested the man who was conjoining these words. A thorough investigation was done. The secret service men considered him (the arrested person) to be a Nazi spy. But the man was innocent. He was only a school teacher and was compiling cross-word puzzles for the paper for the last 20 years. It was a striking case of psychic coincidence.

But perhaps nothing can beat an American experience. The American horror story writer Edgar Allan Poe in his 'The Narrative of Arthur Gordon Pyn' told a story of four famishing survivors of a ship-wreck who finally decided to kill and eat a 12-year old boy, Richard Parkar. Some years later the fiction got transformed into reality. In 1884 a ship was caught in the violent storm and only four people survived. They were also famishing when they decided to kill the cabin boy. The name of the cabin boy who was killed by the senior members of the crew was none other than Richard Parkar.

What was it: a mere coincidence or something else?

The Hidden Treasure

The Oak Island may well be called in R.L. Stevenson's words: 'The Treasure Island'. It was several centuries ago that someone had hidden the money for some mysterious reasons. From 1795 onwards the enthusiasts engaged in the hunt of the treasure have spent a fortune in trying to unravel the mystery of the 'money pit', but to no positive result. A huge amount of money has been wasted, but no 'fortune' has been found. What is the truth?. Why has the treasure remained as elusive as ever?

The discovery of the buried treasure on the Oak Island has a peculiar similarity with the fiction of R.L. Stevenson. In fact the real discovery of the treasure and subsequent efforts to unearth it have every ingredient of 'Naughty Boys Adventure Series'. But, unlike fiction, it does not have a happy end. The story of the search for the buried treasure in the Oak Island began in 1795. Danniel MC Ginnis, who was just 16 years old, had beached his canoe on the south-eastern shore of a small island, Mahone Bay. Daniel liked the environment and went inside the island. While he was seeing the island, he found the fallen oak trees. But amidst them he noticed one tree, a single ancient tree, standing erect. He was intrigued by the same. He called his two friends and soon all the three curious youngsters started digging. And as soon as they started shovelling out the loose earth, they discovered some steps to their utmost shock.

They found circular shafts with hard clay walls which had the marks of picks. But they dug on and after 10 feet of digging they found oak logs embedded in the clay walls. They removed the logs and after 20 feet of digging they again found a clay platform. They realised that it was no ordinary oak tree and that the area was very special and perhaps did something precious.

The three boys then returned to muster up more support but nobody came forward. The people were frightened as the Oak Island had a dangerous reputation for the strange flickering of the lights and the disappearance of men who had gone there to investigate.

Such stories made the three young enthusiasts forget all about the oak treasure for some time. However, after nine years of silence, their thirst got resurged and the three grown-up boys resumed their work in all earnestness. They again started digging but after some feet of digging they repeatedly found platforms of oak which were either unadorned or covered with coconut fibres. After a depth of about 90 feet, they found a flat stone which bore an indecipherable inscription and had strange markings. At that time this discovery was overlooked. It was only half a century later that the stone was exhibited in Halifax. There a professor succeeded in decoding the writing as follows: *"Ten feet below two million pounds"*. Unfortunately, with the advent of the 20th century, the inscription had faded and hence, what that professor had decoded was taken as a gospel truth and the unending search for the Money Pit was accelerated.

However, the excavation started by those three men continued unabated in the 19th century. They dug on till their finance supported them. When their financial position deteriorated, they accepted defeat and returned. For sometime the pit lay undisturbed. It was only after a gap of 44 years that other enthusiasts, desirous of gold, repeatedly took the risk and put their fortune on stake.

One of the shafts leading to the bottomless Money Pit.

But every time their efforts were thwarted by the sudden gush of water which filled the Money Pit frequently. This hide and seek game between excavators and water has continued till this day. No treasure has been unearthed so far. But what surprised the excavators during those times was--how did the water fill the pit?

At Smith's Cove, the treasure-hunters discovered the secret of the flooding of the pit every time they reached a certain level. It is believed that someone dug about 100 feet before 1795. Perhaps, he wanted to hide something very precious. After digging for 100 feet that person constructed a 500 feet tunnel between the shaft and the beach at Smith's Cove. There a pit of plumbing was made which disallowed any entrance to the real hiding place. The shaft was very deliberately and continuously filled so that anybody trying to comprehend beyond that point will not succeed, for the water was to act as the burglar's alarm.

Nevertheless, the various hurdles did not deter the excavators. In 1938 Edwin Hamilton succeeded in excavating a depth of 180 feet. Still success was far away. In addition to the repeated failures, a tragedy occurred in 1963. A retired circus stunt rider was suddenly surrounded by the fumes coming out from the pump, while working in the shaft. His son and two other men jumped in to save his life, but all of them perished. The excavation had to be stopped for the time being. It was four years later that Robert Gunfield, an American petroleum geologist once again took

The aerial view of the Oak Island Money Pit

up the cudgels. He dug an 80 feet wide and 130 feet deep hole near the Money Pit. But, alas, nothing came into his hands!

In 1978 the Triton Alliance Company sunk a submarine television camera into the water-filled cavity. The camera revealed three chests and a severed hand. Divers were lowered to about 235 feet. But once again facts revealed by camera could not be proved. No chest or hand was found.

From the 18th century till the late 20th century, the mystery of the Money Pit has remained unsolved. It appears at this stage that the mystery will remain a riddle for ever. Perhaps, the man who dug the pit prior to 1795 had thought that with the advancement of science and technology in the 19th and 20th centuries, the mystery will be unravelled. But he was certainly mistaken. Till now all efforts have been in vain. The "Money Pit" mystery still remains unsolved. ■

The City of Lord Krishna—Did it Exist?

Is Lord Krishna's Dwarika real or not? For centuries people have held prayers at this place. They have believed it to be a holy city. But in the recent past archaeologists have started talking about another Dwarika situated at another place. Some evidence has been found under the serene blue waters of the Arabian Sea. The search continues still for the Dwarika, the Golden Dwarika, as mentioned in the scriptures. Whether it is a myth or a reality, only time will reveal.

Nowhere else is the need for archaeology to be more precious than in India, where myths and legends abound its history. In the midst of myths and legends, it really becomes difficult to sift facts from fiction. One such character is that of Lord Krishna. His land, Dwarika, was believed to exist in Mathura, but recently some archaeologists have found a few traces of the Golden City in the Arabian Sea.

The archaeologists and historians, who think that Krishna's Dwarika existed in the Arabian Sea, substantiate their view with the following arguments.

According to the epic, the Mahabharata, Kansa was informed about his cruel fate when he was taking his newly married sister, Devaki, and her husband, Vasudeva, back to their home. He was warned that the eighth child of the couple would prove to be the cause of his(Kansa's) death. Believing this incorporeal prediction, Kansa embarked on cruelty towards his sister. He killed all the children of his sister. However, he could not escape his fate. The eighth child, who was later known as Lord Krishna, was saved, and the prophecy was fulfilled by Lord Krishna's killing of Kansa. There was jubiliation everywhere, but in Magadha the father-in-law of Kansa, Jarasandha, swore to take revenge. His repeated attacks compelled Lord Krishna to abandon Mathura. He went to Saurashtra and established Dwarika Nagari on the ruins of the city of Kusasthali, which was established by Revata 200 years ago. Revata was Lord Krishna's ancestor and son of Anarta.

The Dwarika Island

The above text by Harivansa (epilogue to the Mahabharata) further describes Lord Krishna's land overflowing with coconut trees and other vegetation. But as land was not sufficient, a part of the sea was also included in the kingdom and on Lord Krishna's request the sea had retreated.

The story goes that for 36 years the city flourished. And then with the 'mukti' of Lord Krishna, the sea made Dwarika its victim. But Lord Krishna had prior knowledge of the catastrophe. So he had asked Arjuna to vacate the city within seven days after his death. Arjuna obeyed the words of Lord Krishna and as the last batch of the people was going away, the sea water rushed in with great speed and within no time the entire city was submerged. No evidence of any existence was left behind.

So the historians, believing in this part of the story, and finding some significant ancient remains in the sea, were fully convinced that it could be nothing but Lord Krishna's Dwarika. But their critics do not subscribe to this view. They demand concrete evidence pertaining to Dwarika and till some substantial evidence is unearthed, they refuse to accept this explanation.

The believers defend this theory by highlighting the similarity between the lotus marked shell found at this place and its mention in the epic Mahabharata. In addition to this, the protagonists of the theory claim that the various temples found at this place must have been built on the ruins of the old temples. Finally, the supporters say, the Raivataka hill on which Dwarika was situated must be the Barda hills of the present day.

Besides the Mahabharata and the Puranic stories, the Ghata Jataka, composed not later than the third century B.C., also gives a vivid account of Vasudeva and his nine brothers who fought many battles before finally settling down at Dwarika—the beautiful place which had hill on one side and sea on the other. Dr Jayantilal Thakkar, a resident of Dwarika, made a careful study of the area and found remains of the buried houses, pottery, coins and bangles. Taking these as evidences, he stressed that

The Dwarkadhish Temple

Lord Krishna's Dwarika lay under the Dwarkadhish temple or adjacent to it, but was later flooded by sea.

Professor H.D. Sankalia of the Decan College, Pune, believed in the truth of these texts to a certain extent. He excavated a note outside the Dwarkadhish temple in 1963. The excavation continued for several days

The antiquities discovered

and the results brought him nearer to his earlier guess that there existed four habitations, one below the other. But he did not agree that it was Lord Krishna's Golden City. Sankalia merely said, "All discoveries indicate a very ancient civilization." On the other hand, Dr S.S.Rao of the Indian Institute of Oceanography conducted the excavation at the Dwarkadhish temple in 1979. He found the sculptured pillars and plinth of a 12th century temple and also a 9th century temple of Vishnu. Two more temples of an earlier era were also discovered. In fact, much to his amazement, Dr. Rao discovered remains of eight settlements at the same place. The first settlement, he said, must have occurred around 15th century B.C. It revealed that the sea might have caused havoc about 35,000 years ago and that the ruined city must have been Lord Krishna's Dwarika.

The later off-shore excavations further uncovered a huge crescent-shaped bastion and fort walls besides some other structures. All these were discovered within 800 miles of the Samudra Narayan Temple, located near the Dwarka harbour at the Gomati Ghat.

Many antiquities found at the sea shore like conch shells, seals, etc., also suggest the existence of Dwarika, the Golden City, mentioned in the Mahabharata. But whether this Golden City was Lord Krishna's Golden City or not seems difficult to establish.

In the absence of solid archaeological evidence, the mystery of Lord Krishna's Golden City still continues to baffle human imagination. ■

Strange Megalithic Sites of Britain

The sacred Megalithic Sites of Britain are far from being merely relics. They signify the developed ancient technology. In fact, not only technology but research shows that such megalithic structures have mysterious healing powers. These structures are in perfect alignment --a fact that was discovered by chance.

Who discovered the curious alignments? How did he prove his point? How do these structures prove that the technology of the ancients was much more advanced than what is commonly accepted? These are the questions which need deep study.

Alfred Watkins was a respectable Herefordshire brewer. He was little interested in anything else except his work. But one day, their occurred a time-slip and he travelled to his 'ancestral memory'. The journey in the past proved to be very informative. In it he saw a changed

Alfred Watkins who discovered many megalithic sites

countryside burial, a vast stretch of straight lines linking hilltops, mounds, churches and crossroads. He had this astonishing vision in 1921.

At first Watkins did not believe his vision nor did he reveal his vision to anyone. He, rather, sat down with maps and rulers and began to study the topographical features. He checked his vision with the details on the map and finally came to the conclusion that all the sacred megalithic sites of Europe were in a straight line.

The megalithic sites included stone circles which were 900 in number, stone rows, castles and churches and some other standing stones, the oldest of such stones being the Neolithic long barrows and mounds. The castles and churches built along the line offered a wide view of the countryside and were stationed at a defensive position. The intriguing part of the 'ley line', as it has been popularly called (because most of the names of the places on the line end with ley, lay, lee, lea or

The Holy Well of St. Ambrew

A ruined church. Such churches act as 'ley markers'

leigh) is the presence of holy wells at the end of the leys. The holy well of St. Ambrew at Crantock, Cornwall, is quite well known.

We also give below a photograph of a ruined church which acts as a ley marker. Churches were often built on sacred sites.

As usually happens with revelations, so it happened with the ley phenomena as well. Many people refused to believe in the ley lines or alignments. They actively condemned the theory of ley and proposed that in an island as small as Britain, it was but obvious to have a structure in an alignment.

However, there were some who disagreed with this theory.Sir Norman Lockyer, the Astronomical Royal, was the first one to discover the alignment revolving on Stonehenge. He concluded that Stonehenge alignment was in the angle of the midsummer surprise, which were joined to the Neolithic settlement at Grovely castle.

In 1967 Alexander Thom, Professor Emeritus of Engineering Science at Oxford, surveyed more than 600 megalithic sites in Britain and France. After a very detailed and meticulous study he concluded that the prehistoric man had deliberately laid them in an astronomical alignment. With Thom's conclusion, many archaeologists and disbelievers, who had any reservations about ley lines earlier, started believing in the theory of alignment. Gradually a drastic change took place in the thinking of the masses.

After a general somersault in thinking about ley lines, the next bombshell was the acquisition of knowledge about the secret powers of

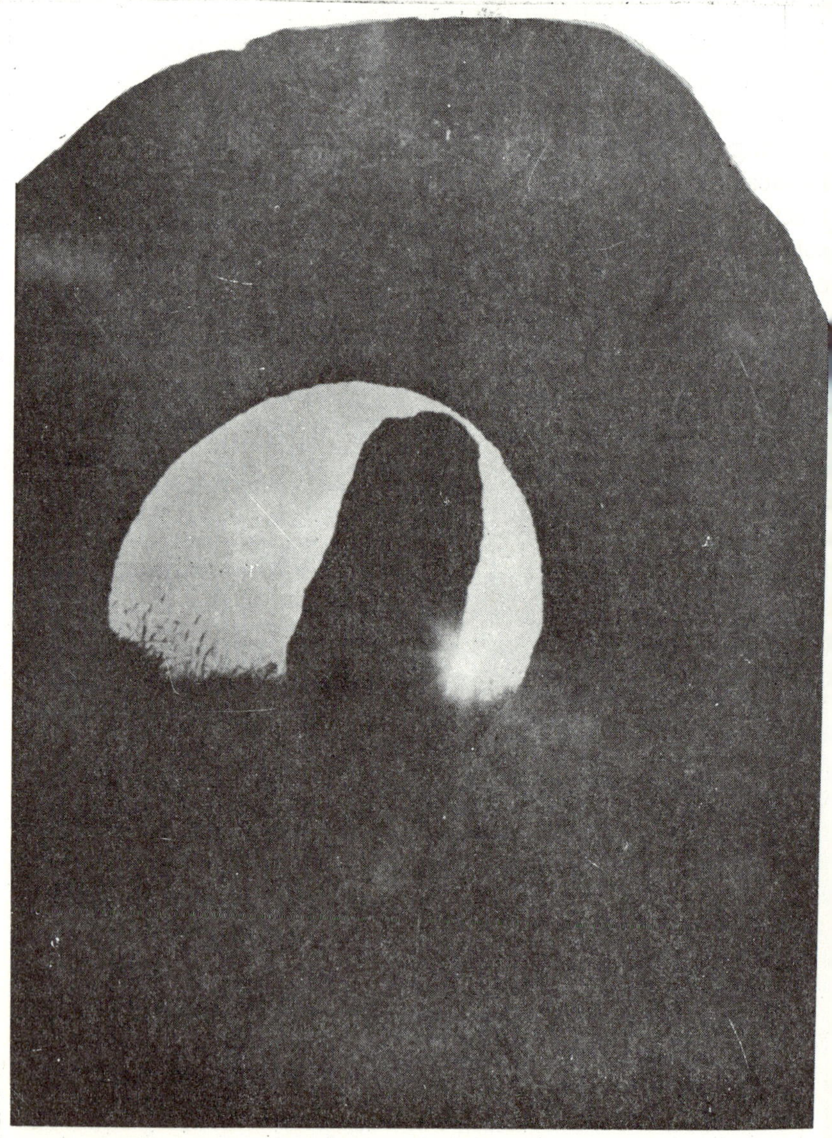

The 'Stone of the Hole'. It has strong healing powers.

the ley stones. Hundreds of ancient stones were found to be possessing some healing powers. The most famous of such stones is the Stone of the Hole, often called Men-an-tol. It is situated at the one end of a Cornish ley. Like so many other megalithic structures, this stone is supposed to be endowed with healing powers. It has cured children suffering from rickets and pricks in the neck. But the healing power only affects if a sick person is able to pass through the hole and then go round the stone. Besides having healing quality, the standing stones and stone circles have worked miracles in ensuring fertility of both women and crops. The standing rocks have also reactivated the psychic powers. Some of the medical men of the Sioux Indian tribe had their psychic powers reactivated by pressing their spines against the wall. Often during battles soldiers gained strength and courage by thrusting their fists into the crevice.

Whether these megalithic structures in the ley line have some supernatural powers or not, is difficult to judge. But it is a fact that many people have gained strength and courage, and have been cured of their various diseases and have got rid of their miseries. It is not that only ill and imbecile persons talk about its existence, but even the statisticians, computer programmers, engineers, doctors, psychics and also astro-archaeologists talk about the peculiar ley system. They all have collected facts and figures and have performed several experiments in search of solutions to these problems. But instead of finding answers to the prevailing question, the mysterious megalithic ley alignments of the stones have eluded their grasp and understanding. ■

Of Mind and Metal : Uri Geller Phenomenon

Metal bending is one of the most controversial phenomena. While some dismiss it as mere fraud, others are made to believe it. They have to trust their eyes.
However, Uri Geller is not the only person practising this unusual art. Many such bizarre cases have been reported. After all who are these people? How do they do it? These are some of the questions which defy all rational explanation.

It was November 23, 1973. The people were watching television. There appeared a young man on the screen. He closed his eyes and duplicated a drawing that had been made just before the programme and sealed it in an envelope. Then he bent a fork by gently stroking it. And a fork which was kept on the table began to bend of its own. And by the time the programme ended, studio telephones started ringing. Viewers were also complaining that their forks and spoons had begun to bend.

The man who created such a sensation was none other than Uri Geller. The simple audience believed in Geller's extraordinary power, but sceptics did not. They suspected that he was a big fraud. The editor of the Sunday Times travelled with Geller in a taxi to the airport and asked him to experiment with his own front door key. Geller was not surprised at the proposal. He started stroking the key. And the key bent like a hot ware candle. The editor realised his mistake.

Uri Geller became a sensation overnight. He gained popularity like a pop star. He was respected everywhere. Even in the U.S., where he was mocked at earlier, he was respected.

Despite the sudden overflow of love and adulation, Geller was not left to himself. He became an interesting subject for scientists to experiment with. A die was placed in a closed box and shaken. Geller was then asked to tell which side was on the top. He guessed it right. But he continuously failed in the test of target drawings. In fact, he could never select the right drawings without the presence of the artist who had made them. This fact led the researchers to conclude that telepathy was an important medium for Geller. However, some more scientific tests followed and Geller proved his genius and the world acknowledged his unique gift.

Besides Uri Geller, there emerged several other metal benders like 17 years old Nicholas William, Girard and Belinda H. In fact Belinda was only six years old when she displayed her unique quality. Belinda was quite different. She was more interested in the process of healing than in displaying her unbelievable qualities. At home she nearly cured her grandmother when she was only a child of three years. On various occasions she relieved her parents of pain. Her method of treatment was simple. She merely used to keep her hand on the affected part of the body of the patient and after a few anxious moments, the pain used to disappear.

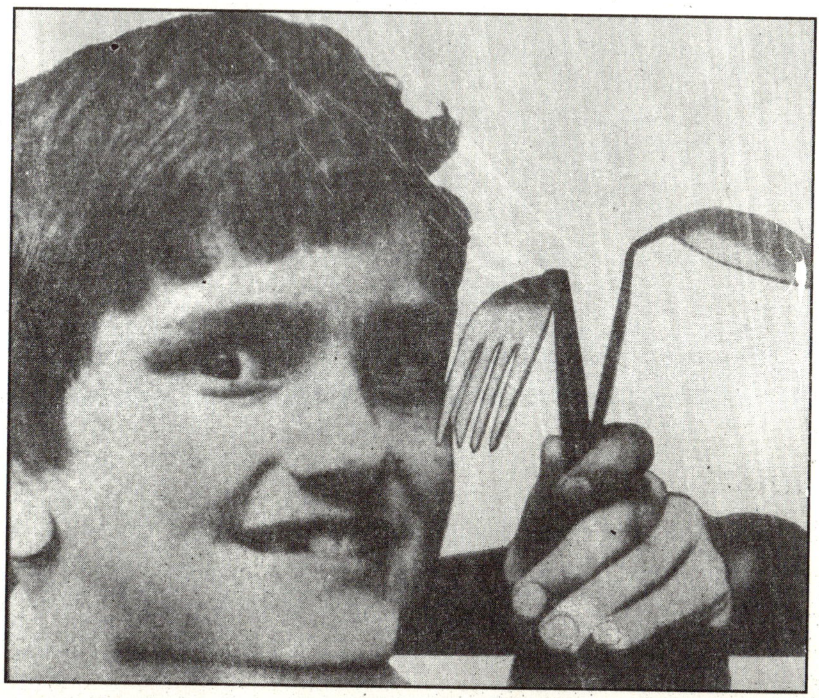

A child displaying the work: both the spoon and the fork are bent.

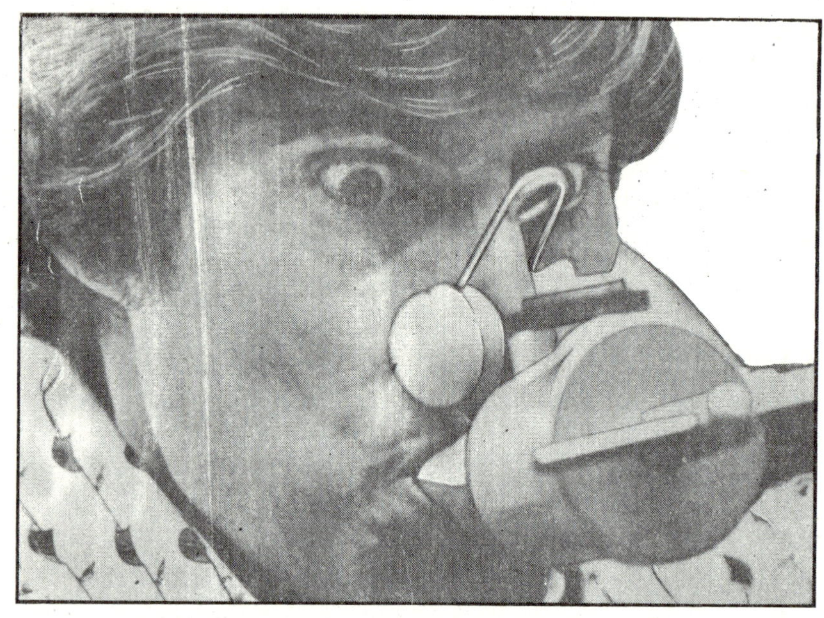

Uri Geller undergoing one of the series of tests to find out if his physical powers were responsible for his mental powers.

The patients used to feel as if they had never been a patient. The cure was miraculous.

No doubt, with its unique mysterious quality, the phenomenon attracted a lot of attention. With the worldwide publicity, the psychiatrists took notice of the incidents with all seriousness. Extensive research was conducted. Dr Robert Cantor, the well known psychiatrist, concluded that youngsters who were gifted with such a quality, suffered from other paranormal abilities. He said that many of these youngsters have reported about the tiny lights moving around them and of high pitched whistles, while some have complained of headaches, particularly while making an effort to bend the metal. And, above all, Cantor said that the children whom he interviewed were frightened that if their power is misused, they will lose it for ever. Hence most of the children were eager to use their exceptional powers for good ends only.

These specially gifted people, Uri Geller, Nicholas William, Girard and Belinda, all require indepth study and cannot merely be dismissed as 'tricksters' or 'frauds'. They are the exceptions, the genius and the superminds. You may even call them magicians. But till the scientists resolve the riddle, this age-old mystery will continue to confound one generation after another. Perhaps it is God's 'gift' to some persons to empower them to relieve others of their pains and miseries. Obviously the healing power granted to their gentle hands, continues to perform miracles relentlessly. The mystery of mind over matter continues to deepen. The scientists, the psychiatrists and the thinkers have still to prove the validity of such phenomena, so that there is left no element of doubt. A day will certainly come when we become familiar with the scientific bases of such happenings.

The Untold Life of Uri Geller

How did Uri Geller come to possess the mystic power? This is a question which has no answer. Geller himself does not know about it. But he admits that he realised his peculiar capability when he was a child of six only. And the first revelation which he told was connected with his mother who had just then returned from a party and had lost quite a lot of money.

When Geller saw her, he immediately knew as to how much she had lost. The realisation about his capability to bend metal came to him, when one day he stared at his watch which was invariably giving incorrect time. He stared at the two hands of the watch and both the hands began to whirl faster and faster. They continued to revolve till he looked at them.. He

Geller with his mother

further realised that his looks or touch would often bend forks and spoons.

By the time he was 13 years of age, he realised the potentiality of his curious powers. During examinations he succeeded in cheating. By concentrating on the back of other intelligent students, he could see the answers written by them.

Geller's parents were quite embarrassed and disturbed. They even took him to a psychiatrist. But the psychiatrist thought about him otherwise. For the noted American psychical researcher, Andrija Puharich, Geller was the "find of the century". He claimed that Geller was the messenger of the Nine, an extra-terrestrial group, which the researchers claim, controls the universe. ■

The Mystery of Fireproof People

Some people are born with mysteries. They can swallow blades, iron, steel or can even walk on fire and nothing happens to them. Such people abound all over the world and exist in every stratum of society. What is their secret? How are they able to achieve such a skill? Questions like these perplex people. And, above all, is the question: how do the people who practise such unique and daring exercises feel?

The villages in India abound in mysteries. A visit to such places makes one shiver. There exist some unique people who excel in performing strange rituals. However, the number of such people is not limited to India alone. They can be found all over the world.

The 'fire walking feat' is most popular among the 'fakirs' of India. On the feast day of the local Hindu deity, they arrive at a village and order a trench to be made and get it filled with hot stones. They then cross the burning trench barefooted and appear at the other end smiling. How are they able to demonstrate such a feat is indeed a mystery to which nobody has been able to give a rational explanation. The only explanation which seems to be somewhat nearer the truth is that the 'fakirs' overcome the pain with their strong will power.

Such daring feats are practised in China, Tibet, Japan and Hong Kong too. In Hong Kong such feats attract a large number of tourists. In Japan, the Shintoism has many fire walking devotees. But the most interesting and baffling aspect of this daring feat is performed by the North American Indians. There the village people prepare themselves for purification by building a roaring fire in the ritual hut. The performers then undress themselves and enter the circle of fire with their leader. The dance follows in which the women often dance around the fire and the men go across the fire. After the dance the leader, called Shaman, takes out the glowing stakes of the wood and applies them on himself as well as on others. Anyone who suffers burns is considered to be in need of extra prayers. However, the ritual does not end with this. After all this is done, each one of them drinks a bowl of salt water. This they vomit into a bowl of sand. Anyone, who fails to vomit, as considered to be impure and undergoes the ritual again. Finally the door of the ritual hut is closed and the Shaman sits round the fire with his followers. They sit till the flames disappear and ashes cool down. The cooled ashes are then mixed with the vomit and left in the open to be blown away. This completes their purification exercise for one year. After a year the ceremony is again repeated. We give below a photograph of the Buddhist fire-walking festival which is held every year at the foot of Mt. Takao in Japan.

The mastery of fire occupies a prominent place in Hinduism. Here the goal of an individual is self-realization which has many stages of development. When an aspirant has successfully gone through these ten or more stages, he achieves the final stage of happiness or bliss. The mastery over fire is an aspect of 'Hatha Yoga' and is achieved with regular practice and exercises to increase one's will-power. Such a person becomes immune to the effects of fire and due to his mastery over fire, his clothes too develop an immunity from fire. These are strange phenomena and surpass the understanding of a human being.

Buddhist fire-walking festival dedicated to prayers for peace.

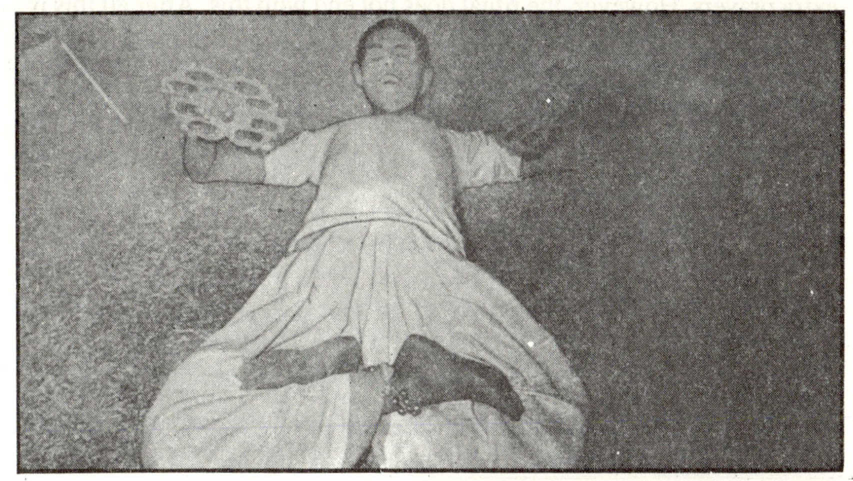

Jatoo Bhai praying before performing the ritual

Bhai dancing in the flames

We will briefly refer to the case of Jatoo Bhai, a saint *(fakir)* from Calcutta who attained such a mastery over fire that he would dance in blazing fire, but would not have any burns after it. Before demonstrating his skill, Jatoo Bhai meditates and offers his prayers to the Almighty. This generates confidence in him so that he could walk on fire without having any burns.

The ritual is not confined to walking on fire alone. When the climax is reached, Jatoo Bhai dances amidst flames in an attitude of ecstasy. His will-power increases tremendously when he performs this ritual.

After the dance was over the feet of the *fakir*, Jatoo Bhai, were seen and every one found to his surprise that his soles were in tact and there were no burns at all. Remarkably enough, his clothes too were in their normal form and without any burns.

Contrary to the brave and confident performers, the onlookers are often shaky and nervous. Fortunately no major casualty has happened so far. The scientists and doctors are not able to comprehend the power possessed by the fire walkers. The question which they often ask is: how do they remain unscathed while walking across baked stones which have a temperature of about 800 F?

In the 1890s Dr. T.N.Hocken tried to unravel the mystery. He

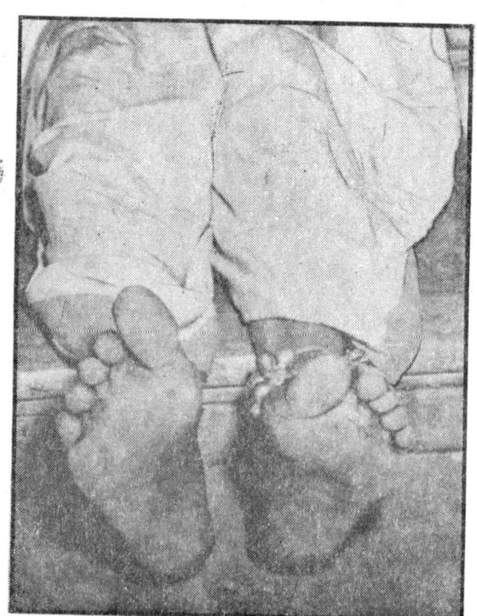

The unburnt feet and clothing of Jatoo Bhai

chemically tested the soles of the fire walkers and also licked them with his tongue. But he did not find any foreign protective substance and eventually absolved them of all charges of trickery.

However, everyone did not agree with Dr Hocken's report. The President of the Folklore Society of England, Edward Clodd, declared in 1895 that the entire exercise was a trickery. He suggested that the feet of such people may have been made insensitive by treating them with sulphuric acid or alum.

Even Clodd's suggestions were rebutted. In 1937 an experiment was conducted at Carlshalton, England. A fiery pit was prepared and there were two participants in the competition. A thorough check-up was conducted. Both the contestants, Ahmed Hussain and Reginald Adcock, had their feet examined before and after the walk. No trickery could be found. The scientists and psychical researchers watched both of them very carefully, but they had to accept the unknown truth that there are miracles which cannot be explained scientifically.

In the absence of any rational and scientific explanation, the fire-proof people continue to parade their unique 'siddhis', or supernatural abilities. Now the owners of success have included such persons amongst their artists. These artists baffle the audience with their dare-devil feats

An artiste depicting immunity from fire :. The phenomenon is real

such as walking on the fire, dancing amidst flames and swallowing the burning flames, without causing the least injury to themselves.

From the above it is clear that immunity from fire cannot be explained on the basis of scientific laws alone. There is a realm of mystery where science does not help us. It will take time before we are in a position to understand the physical and mental changes which take place in a man, while he is demonstrating his 'siddhi' in this regard. ■

The Mask of Time

How can one describe a person who suddenly slips into an alien time and place and after a few minutes' journey returns to the present? Similarly, there are persons who have the capability to leap into the future. However disconcerting these two types of phenomena may be, such incidents are not very common. Some people have no doubt experienced such bizarre incidents of timeslips.
How and why does time behave in such uncharacteristic and strange ways?

Let us look at the experiences of the old man from Norfolk whom we shall call 'Mr Squirrel' for the sake of convenience. His only hobby was collection of coins. He used to keep them in plastic envelopes. In 1973 he went to a particular shop to buy envelopes. He had never visited the shop earlier.Mr Squirrel found the atmosphere of the shop quite peculiar. But before he could further admire the unique atmosphere, a young girl approached him.He asked the young girl for the special envelopes to keep his coins. She produced envelopes from a box full of strange objects and told him that the men on the sailing ships used to buy such envelopes and used them as receptacles for fish hooks. He paid the girl and came out.

After a week Mr Squirrel again went there to buy some more envelopes. This time he got a shock of his life. The place had completely changed. The exterior and interior of the shop were dark and dilapidated. Moreover, the salesgirl was not a young girl but a mature woman.When he enquired about the girl, the staff begged their ignorance. And when he asked for those particular envelopes which he had bought earlier, he was given a negative reply. He was told that such envelopes, were never stocked.

'Mr Squirrel' was shocked. He checked the date of manufacture of those envelopes and was surprised to see that the envelopes were really

The shop in Great Yarmouth, England, where 'Mr Squirrel' went to buy plastic envelopes to keep the coins which he had collected.

antique pieces. They were manufactured before the First World War. Thus it was a case of timeslip, the force of past over the present. He had stepped into another age.

Timeslips into the past is not the only occurrence of this strange phenomenon. There are also future timeslips in which we foresee the future. One day a girl dreamt that her brother is going to have an accident with a red car. The car, the road, the way the accident will occur was completely clear in her dream. And after a few days, the accident took place exactly as she had dreamt.

In another incident a woman continuously dreamt about a big mansion for 20 long years. When one day she visited the beautiful house of Compton Winyates, Warwickshire, England, she immediately recognised it as the object of her dreams.

No consequential meaning is attached to it. The dreamer merely dreamt about it. In fact, it is true that not all dreams are fore-telling. Only some of the dreams predict strange happenings.

At times the precognition can be about the third party. On April 20, 1974, Tersa G. was spending the day with her friend at the White Tower. Suddenly Tersa turned to her friend and said, "I can hear children shouting." Her friend could hear nothing.

A few months later, a terrorist planted a bomb in the armoury of the

The stately mansion, which was the subject of a woman's dream for 20 years, before she actually visited it: Compton Winyates, Warwickshire, England.

White Tower. The bomb exploded and it killed and injured several children and people.

So what was it that Tersa had heard?The psychologists claim that she had heard the agony of children who could suffer in that place some months later.

Anyway, precognition is a widespread phenomenon and has a long history. It is not subject to any human control. The timeslip into the future or precognition of the future does not always have a meaning for the person who experiences it. A person may have a vision about his friend or even some distant relation. The incident foreseen may not take place immediately. It may happen after a few months or some years.

To illustrate this point we may make a mention of the well known psychic, Margaret Baker, who came from East Anglia. She could have a vision of the Olympia bomb disaster much before it actually occurred on March 27, 1976. She even warned her friends not to visit the Ideal Home Exhibition, as she was mightily perturbed by her 'vision'. A day before the explosion took place, she could see with her mind's eye the place where the bomb had been kept. The subsequent television report of the bomb explosion confirmed her vision even to the minutest detail.

Margaret Baker, a psychic from East Anglia

Some Unique Cases

On May 29, 1973, a Norwich teacher, Mrs Anne May visited the Clava Cairns in Inverness. There were three Burial Cairns dating back to the early Bronze Age (1800 - 1500 B.C.). Mrs Anne leaned against a stone and closed her eyes. A moment of darkness occurred. When she opened her eyes, she found herself among a group of men, wearing shaggy tunics and long dark hair. However, with the inflow of tourists and the consequent noisy atmosphere, she returned back to her present existence. The glorious vision ceased.

Now we go to the other case. A child was playing in front of her grandmother's house. Suddenly she ran inside the house and to her amazement, she found herself in a strange environment. Everything was different and everything seemed darker than usual and unnaturally quiet. The girl thought that she had entered a wrong house. So she ran out. But after a few minutes, she again entered the same house. This time everything was all right. Everything was found at its proper place.

The girl had obviously slipped into the past. The timeslips into the past relate to possible reincarnation experiences and to some it is nothing but 'a type of h..unting'. But what exactly happens when one suffers from a timeslip is still a mystery. Probably, such happenings have some

A bronze age burial site, where a visitor entered into a different world, 2,000 years ago.

connection with the human magnetic field. The timeslips, whether they relate to the past or to the future, at least lead to the conclusion that "clock-time" alone is not adequate to explain the various phenomena, like those that we have outlined above. ■

The Monsters in The Water

The seas and lakes often give nightmares to people. The serene vast stretch of water often becomes turbulent. The people walking near the shore often witness strange sights. They see some giants which apparently are neither animals nor human beings. Then what are they ? This is the question which many ask.

Many stories and myths surround lakes and rivers. Some of the stories about evil water monsters are so prominent that legends have been woven around them. And since these demons were made to appear like horses, the other name attributed to them is horse-eel.

The monsters existed during earlier centuries too. A story goes that during the 12th century a monster lived in a lake in Ireland. This beast emerged from water only to take meals. And its meals consisted of the people and cattle living nearby. Once a brave Irish hero, Cuchulain, was close by. But when he heard the monster coming, he, unlike a hero, saved his life only. Another legend goes that a poor girl, while washing her clothes, was eaten up by the monster. Such legends are widespread. And they did not disappear in the 12th century, but their echoes can be heard even now in the 20th century.

An extinct plesiosaur was seen in the Indian Ocean in 1938. That it was supposed to have disappeared 70 million years ago did not discourage the people in believing in this sea-giant.

In 1982 Mrs Dilys Fisher, a teacher by profession, saw the monster in Loch Ness, a lake which divides the Highlands of Scotland and is connected to the sea by the river Ness. Describing the scene later on she said, "There is obviously something very large in water moving at great speed close to the shore. Initially, I could see the black Hump-like object but it remained submerged. Then within seconds I could see two objects, one which I took to be the tail. I watched spell bound.........the creature dived deeply, creating a considerable displacement of water and disappeared."

Plesiosaur, the reptile which is believed to have been extinct for the past 70 million years. But in 1938, it was spotted in the Indian Ocean. The minute details fit into the description of the Loch Ness Monster.

Just four years after this incident, three teenaged girls were working at the Loch Ness hotel, when they suddenly saw a dark shape. One of the girls later commented that despite the huge shape, no sound was produced. "Yet", she affirmed, "it could not have been an illusion because we all saw it."

The recent sightings again sparked the decaying interest in Loch Ness monster. The interest became so prominent that in 1984 a tubular trap (80 feet long) made out of fibre glass was airlifted into the Loch. The curious men waited for a reward. They wanted to photograph the monster for examination. But their long patience was not rewarded.

Lake Hanas in China also gave birth to many monster stories. The technicians of Xinjiang University travelled to the lake situated in between the thickly forested mountains in 1980. Their efforts did not completely go a waste. They saw 'a large red shape' which disappeared as suddenly as it had appeared.

In 1982, a Polish newspaper, Kurter Polski, wrote the experience of a young swimmer in Zegrczynski lake. The newspaper wrote that the boy saw a huge beast "with rabbit like ears."

In Russia, people have continuously complained about the strange animals sighted at Lake Kol-Kol. So much so that some eye-witnesses strongly believe that the strange animal is nobody else but a dinosaur. But

A monster covered with bristles and having a hippo-like face with a horn

some disagree. According to them the monster had a twisty body about 20 metres long.

Monsters were not sighted in large lakes only. Even in small lakes 'giant fish', 'living trunk' or the 'horse like head' monsters have been sighted. However, the most astonishing myth which has floated since long is the mystery of Loch Ness monster, which has attracted many researchers. In 1983 a book was published entitled, 'The Loch Ness Mystery Solved'. The authors of the book, Ronald Binns made it quite apparent that there is no such thing as monster in the lake. They explained that all eye-witness accounts can be traced far back in history. According to them the often sighted monster is nothing but a neolithic carved stone which has a pictish design. Some other sightings they label as 'mirages'.

Binns and Bell were not the only one to disagree with the accepted fact. Even Steuard Campbell of Edinburgh who analysed and dissected the print of the 'Surgeon's photograph' concluded that the mystery of the monster was nothing. According to him the photograph shows nothing but a boat.

Whether Loch Ness sighting is a monster or not is difficult to

The 'Surgeon's Photograph'

answer. But one fact seemingly appears very clearly that the world wants to believe in the myth of monsters. And till the myth is rationally and logically explained and supported with hard facts, the stories will continue to germinate. The mystery will remain frightening and puzzling.

Some Strange Sightings

It was the year 1966. A man was fishing in Lough Attariff. Suddenly a long dark brown object surfaced. This object was 100 yards away from him and according to him, it had the head of a well grown calf and a pair of large glittering eyes. After a few minutes, it disappeared. Then in 1967, this very man again saw a light yellowish brown monster, about 7 feet long at another place in Lake Lackogh in County Kerry.

In 1979 two farmers saw a reptilian creature which was completely black and about 10 feet long. In 1980 in Canada; a unique, unseen pair of creatures was spotted in Saddle Lake and Christina Lake. The viewers said that their heads were shaped like horses, eyes were as large as saucers and they had hair on their body too.

In 1982 a Polish boy claimed that he was confronted by a beast while he was swimming in Zegrzynski Lake. He described the beast as having an enormous slimy black head with rabbit like ears. ■

Does Hypnosis Exist?

Hypnosis is one field which, like astrology, has attracted a lot of attention. It has both astute believers and hard core critics. There are some who believe that it is one of the ancient sciences while the bitter critics disagree. For them it is nothing more than a faux pass.

What is hypnosis then ? How have doctors performed operations without putting patients under anaesthesia? Is hypnosis the answer? What is this baffling hypothesis which has aroused so much controversy?

A depressed man visits a hypnotherapist. The doctor listens to the patient's grouses sympathetically. While listening, he is constantly looking into the eyes of the patient. After narrating a few details of his mundane life, the patient enters into another world. He becomes a puppet of his environment. No longer is he disturbed by the pain and pangs of depression. But this state does not remain for ever. Soon the hypnotherapist brings him back to the rigmarole of the cut-throat world.

The patient returns home, but only for a few hours. His frequent visits to the doctor become a part of the usual course of his life.

The popularity of hypnotism has reached its zenith in the 20th century. In late 1920s various operations were performed without inducing anaesthesia to the patients. A French doctor, A.A. Liebeault, tried hypnotherapy on his patients. The experiment was successful and it was inducted into the hospital's routine treatment.

Nonetheless, sceptics refused to believe that there is any science such as hypnotherapy. They believed that it was nothing but connected with hysteria, which the non-believers categorically stated was not to be believed. The doctors too shied away from it.

It was only in the second half of the 20th century that a great deal of attention was drawn towards it. It became a serious subject of study. Various books were written and TV programmes were conducted. The

A hypnotised chicken : Its beak is forced down to a chalk line. Obviously the chicken feels that it cannot move away from the line.

grey views were then smeared with positive colours. The two books which really created a lot of impact were 'More Lives Than One' and 'Encounters With The past'. The former is written by a BBC producer, Jeffrey Iverson and the latter by Peter Moss.

The best known experiment was conducted by the late Arnall Bloxham. He regressed Cardiff housewife, Jane Evans. And when regressed, she became a 12th century Jevess, Rebecca. Under hypnosis she narrated her life in detail. She gave a crypt description of the church and the Jewish massacre. Her descriptions were found to be *cent percent* accurate.

Hypnotism is something which is not only experimented on human beings, but also on animals. The classic example of hypnotism is that of a chicken whose beak was forced down to a line drawn by a chalk. The chicken too, till it was under hypnosis, believed that it could not move away from the line. The critics were indeed astonished to see such a magnitude of hypnosis.

Then came its usage in the police department. So accurate were the descriptions provided by the hypnotised people that soon police also inducted this method in finding out the culprit. There is a case of an Israeli girl who was brutally raped, but unfortunately had no recollection of the attacker. However, when she was put under hypnosis, she gave a vivid

Arthur Ashe-An American Tennis Star. He used post-hypnotic suggestions to enable him to give his best.

description of the culprit. With the help of her descriptions under hypnosis, the police was able to locate the rapist and punish him.

In the recent past, hypnosis has also been used by players like Bob Willis (Fst Bowler), Roslaine Few (champion high jump of the early 170s) and Arthur Ashe (tennis star) all took post-hypnotic treatment to enable them to display their best in their respective games.

Nonetheless, there are still many researchers and scientists who disagreee with the concept of hypnosis. According to them it does not exist. And since the protagonists themselves do not know the mechanism by which hypnotic spell is cast, the queries of the non-believers remain unanswered.

But it is true that operations have been performed under hypnosis without anaesthesia and the patients have not experienced any pain or agony of an operation. It is also true that the mysteries of murders and rapes have been resolved with the help of hypnosis. The patients have been cured of their untold traumas and sufferings.

How such facts have been accomplished, nobody knows. An air of mystery surrounds the experiments of hypnosis.

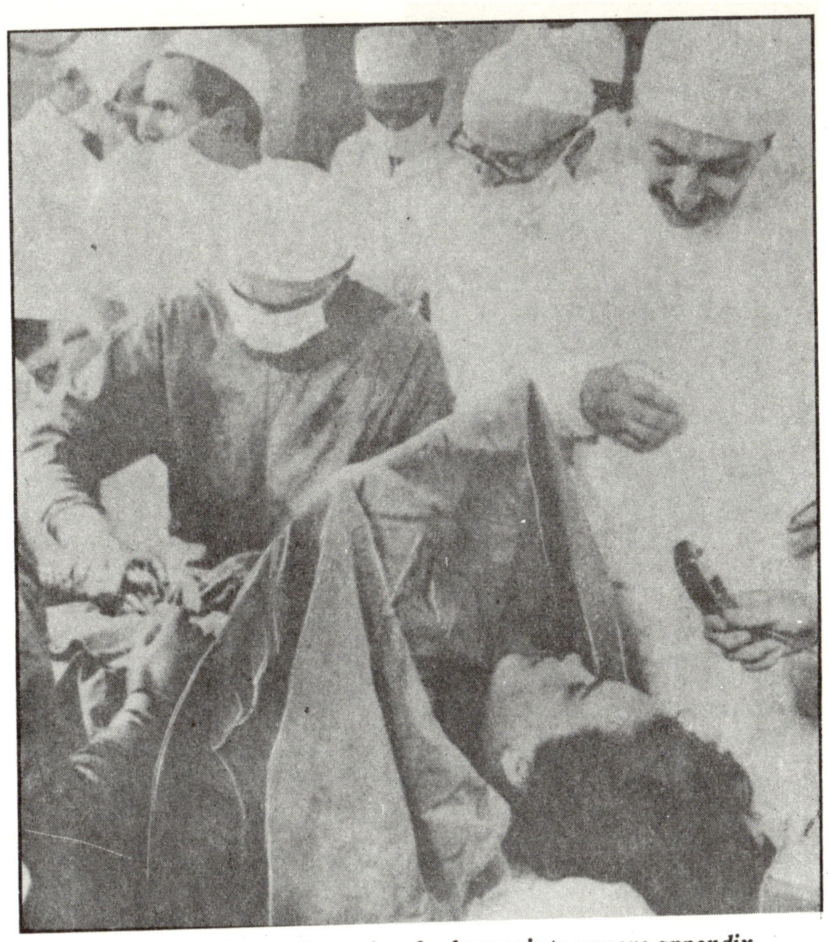

Operation being performed under hypnosis to remove appendix.

Bizarre case of Hypnotism

In 1976 some people in France complained of insomnia. They visited Jacquy Nuguet, a hypnotherapist. He did a miracle under medical supervision. He put all the patients under 'mass sleep'. They slept continuously for 10 days and got up only for a short while to attend to their daily needs and to take a little bit of orange juice. The experiment was successful. All the patients were cured of insomnia. The medical scientists had no answer to this experiment.

In the end we can say that, "The indisputable fact is that there is a state of mind.........which can be induced by a variety of

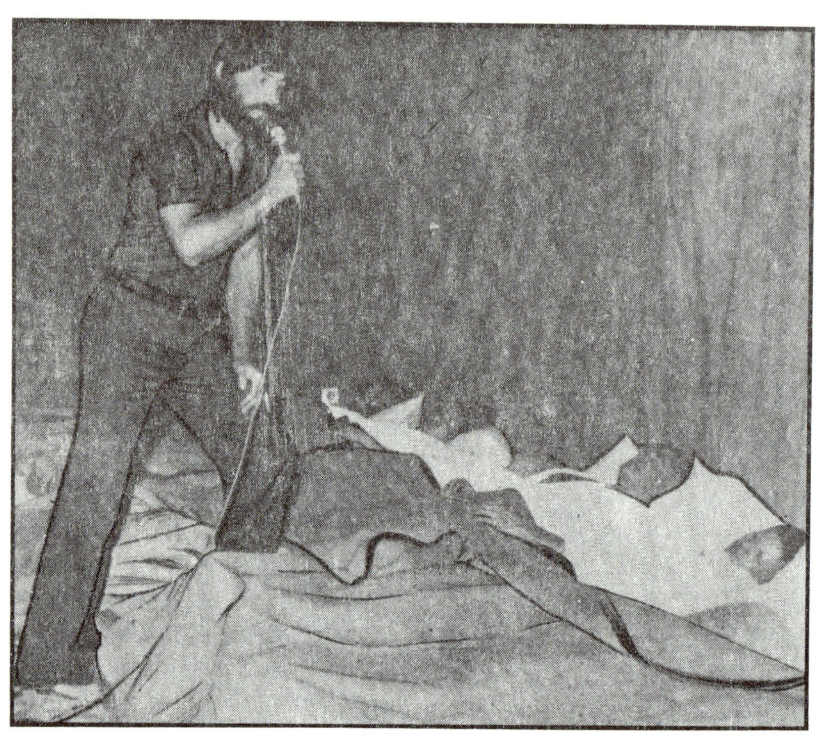

Mass hypnotism by Jacquy Nuguet. This feat was performed in France in 1976.

techniques.........during which some individuals appear to enjoy remarkable faculties and capabilities.".........."Some subjects also become highly suggestible—dropping the defences that normally they would put up............" ■

Whose Footprints are These?

In February 1855 a trail of peculiar footprints was discovered in South Devon, England. This single straight line of tracks was in the snow. No one could tell whose marks were those and what had caused them? But to some those hoofmarks were nothing but the devil's footprints. The scientists do not agree on this point. Hence the question arises: Whose footprints are these?

The winter of 1855 was too severe. England was in the grip of an exceptionally icy wave. The river Thames was frozen at Kingston and the isolated villages in the west England were cut off by flurries of snow. People were out of work because of the icy conditions and many travellers perished in the freezing temperature.

February 8th was like any other cold winter day for the inhabitants of Devon. But the description of an uncommon sight given by Albert Brailford, the school Principal of Topsham village in Devonshire, could no longer let the curious inhabitants remain inside the house. They charged out and were intrigued to see a peculiar line of footprints in the snow. The footprints were shaped like horseshoes. Each was about 4 inches long and looked as if it had been made by a hoofed animal. The marks measured from an inch and a half to two and a half inches across.

The villagers were frightened. Being superstitious they thought that the marks were left by Satan itself. The mystery deepened as the villagers discovered that the marks at some places went over rooftops. Such tracks continued for 40 miles along the South Devon coast. In one village the marks stopped at the door of a shed and reappeared at the back of it, emerging from a six-inch hole. Then the prints went up to a haystack, disappeared and were resumed on the other side. Despite their sudden appearance and disappearance the tracks were always found to be in a straight line.

The news was peculiar and inevitably newsmen and eager scientists

The Kerguelen Island which lies close to the Antarctic circle was visited by a British expedition in 1840. The footprints were found there too. It was called the 'island of desolation'.

appeared on the scene. They gave their personal versions.

A Devon Vicar and naturalist denied that there was a supernatural force behind the footmarks. As the tracks always measured eight and a half inches, it was very well understood that it could be the work of only one creature. But the question which the Vicar could not answer related to the animal which could have presumably walked over 80 miles from dusk to dawn, climbed over roofs and walked through haystacks. But Sir Richard Owen, the famous naturalist examined the tracks and opined that they were made by a badger. A badger is a burrowing nocturnal animal of the otter and weasel family and is a strong and untiring creature. But very few naturalists accepted his theory.

Sir Richard Owen, a leading naturalist of 19th Century, who expressed his considered opinion that the footprints were those of a badger, a nocturnal creature that 'comes abroad occasionally in the late winter when it is hard-pressed by cold and hunger'.

A badger well known for its untiring nature

Some of the naturalists said that it must have been the work of a local prankster. But even this explanation did not satisfy the observers. The observers questioned as to how did it jump over the walls and climb the rooftops, and cover 80 miles just in a single night?

Some keen observers were eager to point out that it was not the only

Sir James Clark Ross who had discovered single-track prints in the snow.

case of prints in the snow. According to a newspaper, 'The Western Times', a similar occurrence took place in 1850, five years before the one in Devon. Inspired by the newspaper's revelation many observers declared that in 1840, Captain Sir James Clark Ross, while on expedition to Antarctic, witnessed the unidentified traces in the snow at Kerguelen Island. As late as 1945, the science fiction writer, Eric Frank Russell, while serving with the Allied Army, reported having seen similar marks in the snow. Russel later wrote that local people feared to talk about it.

Indeed after so many years, it is impossible to come to a correct and valid conclusion for no longer those footmarks are available for close examination. On the other hand, it is true that mysterious footprints on that shivering winter night gave rise to many superstitions. Yet the vital question: "Whose footprints are these?" could not be answered correctly till this day. The mystery, may perhaps never be resolved, as there is no end to human speculations. ■

Born Never to Die

Some extraordinarily sensitive people loudly proclaim that they are continuing the work of long dead acclaimed creative genuises. They give their latest work to the world with a word that 'it was not me who wrote it, but.........'. The blank can be filled in by the names of great persons such as Beethoven, Liszt, Chopin, Schubert or Stravinsky.

What does it mean? Are these people a farce or is their work the result of their subconscious mind? Or else, have the graves turned up?

An unassuming middle aged London housewife has a very little knowledge of music. Yet she produces extraordinary and incredible

Mrs. Rosemary Brown

work. Rosemary Brown—that's her name, sees herself as the humble scribe and friend of the late composers. The final touch to her master-pieces are indeed given by the professionals.

Rosemary had little interest in music till she became a widow and saw a picture of Franz Liszt and recognized him as her ghostly friend. Liszt lived a century earlier i.e., from 1811 to 1886.

Then in 1964 Rosemary claims that she was contacted by the famous composers like Beethoven and Chopin. This was a turning point in Mrs Rosemary Brown's exciting life. She became serious about her work. The fully composed pieces of music were transmitted to her. "My job was just to write it down as fast as I could", explained Rosemary Brown about her unique gift. "At times", she further said, "the communication is interrupted because they would become so excited that they would start speaking in their native language i.e., in Polish or German." She wrote down their words phonetically and later had them translated by a Polish friend.

After Rosemary's 'taking down the notes', her works were passed on to the living music giants, like Menuhim, Rodney Bennet and others.

Beethoven who contacted Rosemary Brown in 1964

A pen and ink drawing produced through the hands of Mathew Manning. The style is that of Aubrey Beardsley's.

And all of them were surprised to see the maturity of the person who literally had no formal training in music.

However, Rosemary Brown's journey was not confined within the four walls of 'music' only. She also declared that she had been visited by dead artists poets, playwrights, philosophers and scientists. Vincent van Gogh (1853-1890) apparently made his latest art work through her. Bertrand Russel, according to Rosemary, is still 'alive' and wants to pass on the message of hope in eternal life. She is also regularly in touch with Albert Einstein.

Rosemary Brown is not the only 'gifted' woman. There are many others. Mathew Manning, a British Psychic, produced a painting by Pablo Picasso, three months after the latter's death in 1973. Mrs Pearl

Aposthumous Picasso : A painting by Mathew Manning. It may be recalled that Picasso was one of 'the few artists who chose to use colour'

Curran was amanuensis of Patience Worth and produced prize winning literature.

It is interesting to note that Mathew Manning used colour in his paintings just in the spirit of Picasso. The following photograph may be seen in this connection.

Is this kind of work merely the exhibition of the dead finding their own repressed creativity ? Or is it really, as psychics would let people believe, that the world's great musicians, writers and artists are trying to prove their continual existence by carrying on their work through selected sensitive?

These are some of the questions which baffle the psychologists as well as the public. Nobody has been able to find the answers to these mysterious happenings.

Meanwhile, the media of creative geniuses continue to churn out remarkable art pieces. Frank Leah, Coral Polge and Margaret Bevan have produced drawings of the 'spirits' with startling likenesses.

Perhaps all these incidents only point out that there is no death and life of a genius who is 'eternal'!

Who was Patience Worth?

Patience Worth was often invited to literary receptions, but she always sent her regrets.

She produced numerous literary works. Her novel entitled 'The Sorry Tale' which comprised 3,00,000 words. was dictated every evening, over a period of two years. This novel revealed scholarly knowledge of Biblical lands and customs. Readers liked it, but one question haunted them: who wrote it? Mrs Curran, who virtually acted as the secretary taking down the dictation, hardly had any knowledge of literature herself.

Quite surprisingly, Patience Worth was compared to Keats, Browning, Brontes and Shakespeare. But who she was, nobody knows. The whereabouts of the author of 'The Sorry Tale' are a mystery. ■

The Mysticism of Suffering

Some deeply religious Christians suffer the way Christ suffered. Their bodies develop wounds. They bleed. Why do they do it? What is this curious phenomenon of stigmata? Do not their bodies ache?

There are many such questions which are best left for mysticism to answer.

Gemma Galgani was an orphan. She was 23 years old and passionately wanted to become a nun. But Nature did not allow her to wear white clothes. She was patient of spinal tuberculosis. So she accepted her fate quietly and became a domestic helper. But she did not forget her ambition. She prayed regularly and was a devout believer in God.

Once while praying before a large crucifix, Gemma experienced a vision that changed the course of her life. The next day when her mother opened her room, she shrieked with horror. Gemma's arms and back were covered with marks like those of whipping and her clothes were soaked in blood. This was the beginning of stigmata. It occurred every Thursday and vanished the next day. The wounds used to close on Friday and left behind only a whitish mark.

This happened in 1901. The earliest reported stigmatic case occurred centuries ago in 1224. St. Francis of Assisi was stigmatised while in a spiritual retreat on Mount Alvernia in the Italian Apennines. But since 1901 many stigmatic cases have been reported.

A Spanish mystic and self appointed 'Pope', regularly developed stigmata such as the crown of thorns and the side wounds during 1970s.

Padre Pio Fortgione was stigmatised in 1915 at the age of 28. Since then he was continuously stigmatised till his death in 1968. He was one of the most respected stigmatics. His hands were pierced through and he suffered from constant pain in his hands. But he never complained and possessed remarkable capacity for endurance.

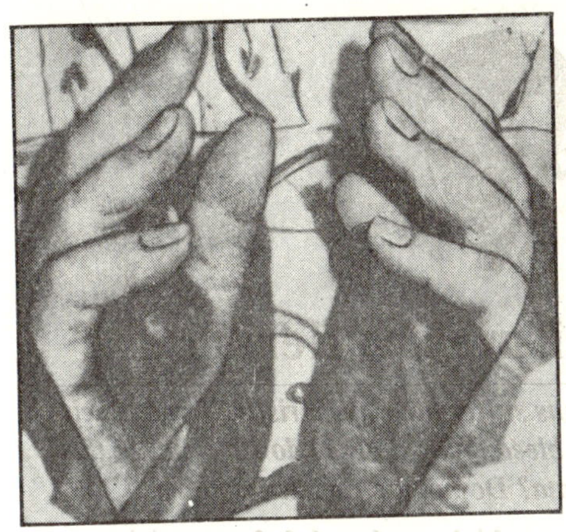

The hands of Padre Pio Forgione

Teresa Neumann was a poor Bavarian and suffered from incurable illness. She was stigmatised in 1926 and continued to be stigmatised till her death in 1962. Wounds appeared upon her hands, sides and on her forehead. She lost weight tremendously. Various doctors examined her and confirmed the astonishing fact. More surprising to the medical

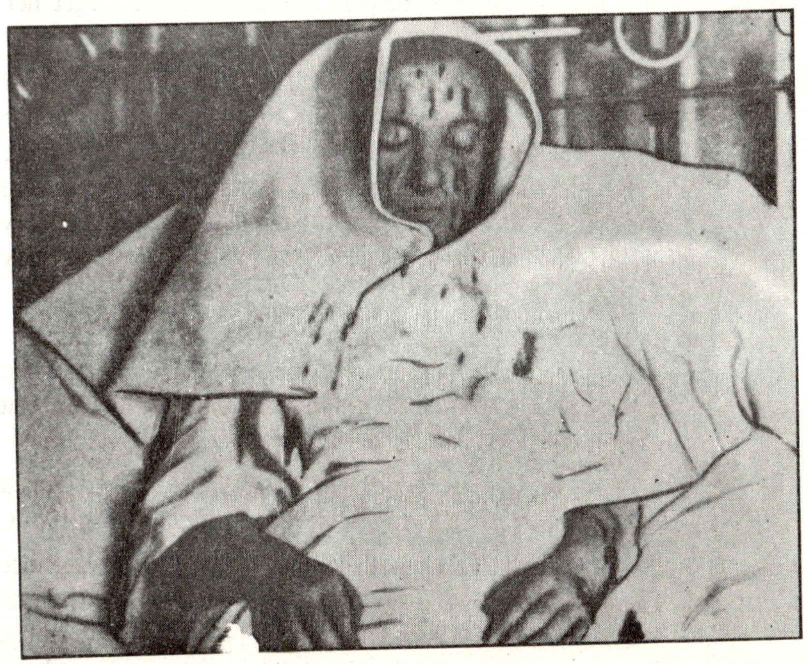

Teresa Neumann

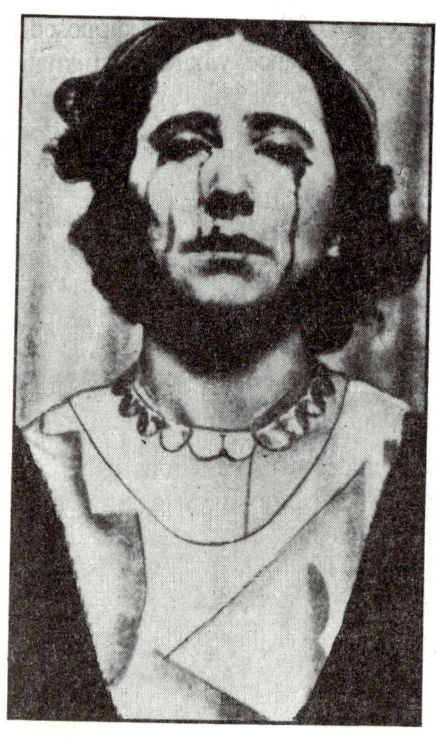

A true stigmata : the mystery surrounds such a phenomenon even to-day

science was the fact that she stopped passing excreta and her intestines decayed, yet she lived long.

A 10 year old, Cloretta Robinson, was stigmatised in 1972. She lived for nineteen days after being stigmatised. Her case aroused a lot of curiosity because she was a non-catholic black stigmatic. There is another case of a person who used to weep 'blood', which was considered to be a sign of true stigmata.

Such peculiar stigmatic cases continue to happen even in this decade. The questions that arise in this connection are: Who are stigmatics and what does the word 'stigmata' mean?

The word 'stigmata' means and signifies the wounds suffered by Christ during his arrest, trial and execution. A person who suffers from stigmata also gets wounds on various parts of the body. And the blood that flows from them is clean arterial blood without any trace of disease. The wounds at times do remain open for long periods, but do not get infected. Much to the surprise of medical science these wounds appear and disappear themselves. The appearance of these wounds supposedly depends upon the state of consciousness to trance, where the stigmatic experiences a union with the sufferings of Christ.The stigmata usually happens during Easter or Church feast days or on Friday, particularly Easter Friday known as Good Friday.

This has been especially found to occur amidst the members of the Roman Catholic Church. The Church as such has no substantial answer to the cause of stigmata. The medical science has also failed to provide any reason for it and its subsequent healing. Many attempts were made to reproduce stigmata by hypnosis. But the result was disastrous. The wounds reddened the skin and there occurred sporadic bleeding. Moreover, it defied the normal stigmata, where the wound healed itself.

Thus the mystery of the stigmata eludes all explanations to this day. The only possible explanation seems to be that the stigmata effects must be having some connection with the unconscious minds of the stigmatics and the crucifixion of Christ. What actually the reason is, is indeed a mystery. In fact the occurrence of wounds and their healing is a miracle. So far no medical science has been able to explain the phenomena. ■

Bodies that Do not Decay

How is it that some people preserve dead bodies for years and years together? Not long ago a woman in India preserved the dead body of her husband for 12 long years. She not only preserved the body, but she bathed it daily and even slept in the same room. The case was too bizarre. It shook the tender sensibilities of the people. The press reported exhaustively on it and the woman was sent for a medical check-up.

This is not the only case in the world. There are many others. What then is the reason for preserving a dead body and how do people do it?

A little girl named Nadja Mattei died in 1965 in Rome. She was just two years old at the time of her death. Her mother put the body into a coffin. But for 12 years she continuously dreamt that her daughter was begging to be taken out of the coffin. So the devoted mother tried to convince the authorities to let her open the coffin. But all her efforts were futile till 1977, when finally the exhumation of Baby Nadja was granted. And to every one's surprise, the body was found to be completely free from rotting.

A similar incident occurred at Kano North of Nigeria. A heretical muslim cult was led by a self-styled prophet, Muhammadu Marwa. He had established himself in 1960s and had a vast number of followers. But seemingly everything was not as peaceful as it should have been. The orthodox muslims were against him. Finally the brewing tension exploded in December 1980. A fierce riot took place in which as many as 8,000 people were killed. The heretical Muslim sect leader was also killed.

His followers buried him in a shallow grave. But because of the immense respect that he commanded, three weeks later the Governor gave orders that his body be exhumed and placed on ice in the city mortuary. Even after remaining buried for three weeks, the body did not decay. The people thought that it was a miracle.

Marwa, the self-styled Prophet. He had about 10,000 followers.

The oldest 6470 year old mummy of 'The Young Lady of Loulan'

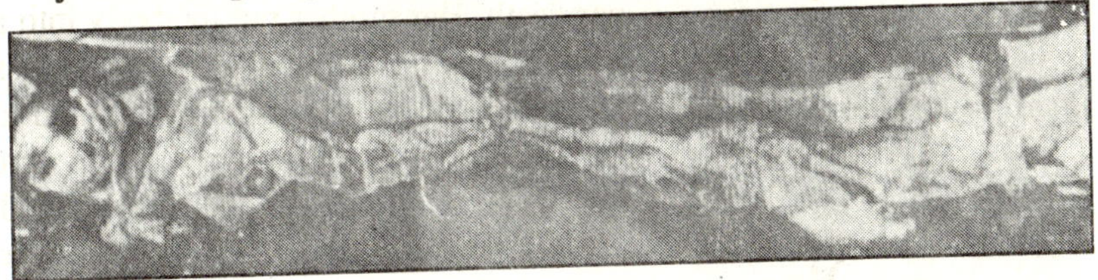

There are innumerable other cases. There was unearthed a mummy of the 'young lady of Loulan' in Xinjiang province of China in 1981, which is claimed to be the oldest mummy in the world.

The question invariably arises: if such cases are not miracles, what is the reality about them?

Often the sceptics believe that bodies would have been embalmed. But this is not completely true. The medical examination of these bodies testified that no preservatives were used and none of the viscera had been removed. John Cruz wrote a book about these phenomena entitled "The Incorruptibles". There he described three types of preserved bodies. "Those preserved deliberately; the accidentially or naturally preserved, and the true incorruptibles." He extensively cites the cases which were preserved but not in mummified form. He describes the case of a mummy found in a mountain cave in Chile in 1954, which was supposed to have been dragged and left there to freeze as a token of sacrifice. This incident is reported to have occurred some 500 years ago. Cruz also gives examples of the people of Iron Age who have been found preserved in peat bogs in Denmark, Ireland and Scotland, though the bodies found at these places were discoloured by natural chemical processes.

Furthermore, the sites for burial are at times chosen in such a way that decompostion is delayed. The case of the Capuchin monks hanging like broken dolls in the catacombs in Palermo, Sicily, is well-known. The bodies of the monks have not decayed although they were left exposed to the air. It was discovered that the air in these catacombs has the peculiar property of drying out the bodies and turning them into natural mummies.

The vaults of St Michan's Church, Dublin, seem to have the same peculiar quality. In 1901 a survey was done and a body of a pathetic baby-

The Capuchin Monks. A 19th entury traveller wrote about them : "They are all dressed in the clothes they usually wore......the skin and muscles become as dry and hard as a piece of stockfish, and though many of them have been here upward of two hundred and fifty years, yet none are reduced to skeletons."

corpse was discovered at this place. The faded white ribbons of the funeral were visible on the round plump wrists of the baby. The date mentioned on the coffin was 1679. The scientists explained that the preservation was caused by the extreme dryness of the air and its freedom from dust. Such conditions prevail even in Kiev in Russia and many withered bodies lie in open coffins.

It is true that there is something in the air which protects the body and keeps them intact. But it is also a fact that some bodies do decay and rot. The religion has its own explanation for this. The Catholic Church looks at it as a 'divine favour' to a pious soul.

However, true incorruption of the body is extremely rare. Most of the stories floated about these phenomena have almost a similar structure. They mention about the persistent fragrance coming out of the incorrupt body and some supernatural accompanying event such as the presence of light around the grave. It, therefore, follows that the nature of reality, its physical and spiritual laws and their interdependence should be thoroughly re-examined, so that the mystery underlying the "incorruption of bodies" be unravelled. Till it is done, such miracles have to be explained and understood on the basis of "faith" and Divine Blessings. ■

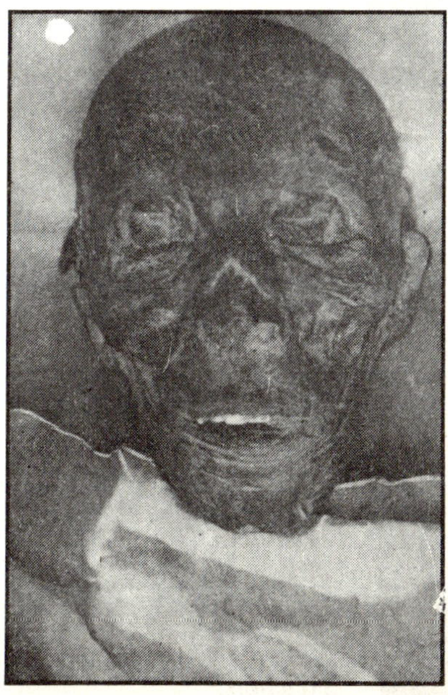

An Egyptian mummy, thousands of years old in Cairo museum.

The Dragon Connection

What is a dragon? Is there such a thing as a dragon on earth? History and mythology answer in the positive. But in the present we do not see any dragon. So, where have all the dragons disappeared? Or was the dragon just an imaginary concept to enable us to rationalise some of the peculiar unanswerable happenings of the world?

The mythologies of almost all countries talk about dragons. It is a different thing that the picture depicted in the Western mythology is completely different from the picture of dragons painted in the Eastern mythology. Many famous legends are woven around dragons.

The story of Essex serpent has been carved in the British Museum, and the Bowe's manuscript at the British museum extensively narrates the encounter with the Sockburn dragon. According to the manuscript, Sockburn dragon terrorises a parish in Durham county during Saxon times.

The dragon phenomenon has been explained by various researchers and scholars in different ways. But none of them could arrive at a point of agreement. In fact, all the explanations were weak. And in the absence of any scientific theory, legend and fantasy inevitably surrounded the dragon myth. Hence it came to be believed that dragon must have been the successor of some real animal.

In 1980, the skull and the jawbones of 150 years ancient animal - Plesiosaur were discovered. Plesiosaur and Pterodactyl are supposed to be the two great sea monsters who existed millions of years ago. The jawbones which were dug out from a claypit in Westbury, Wiltshire, had about 80 teeth. The biggest tooth was 8 inches long and the size of the jaw suggested that the creature must have been thirty feet long.

Some scholars believe that dragons escaped the fate of their relatives. They survived for a long time before finally disappearing. On the other hand a few scholars have suggested that dragons have not

The jaw of a plesiosaur, a sea monster that has been extinct for 150 million years.

disappeared and that they still live. Professor Carl Sagan believes that dragon-legend survives. He substantiates his theory by stating that the fossil unearthed is that of 60 million years ago, while the man and his family (Homo) is of only tens of million years old. On account of these facts he assumes that there must have been a creature similar to man, who probably escaped extinction.

The mythologies abound in stories of dragons. In the West during the middle ages the phoenix was considered to be the symbol of resurrection; panther represented Christ and dragon was the symbol of anti-Christ. The story recounts that whenever panther searched for food, dragon shied away and hid itself. The dragon was too afraid of panther In simpler words the story suggests victory of good over evil.

The famous Roman historian Pliny also talked about the dragon phenomenon exhaustively. In his book 'Histories' written in the first century A.D., he has exhaustively described the enmity between the dragon and the elephant.

Besides the early historians and writers, the cartographers also

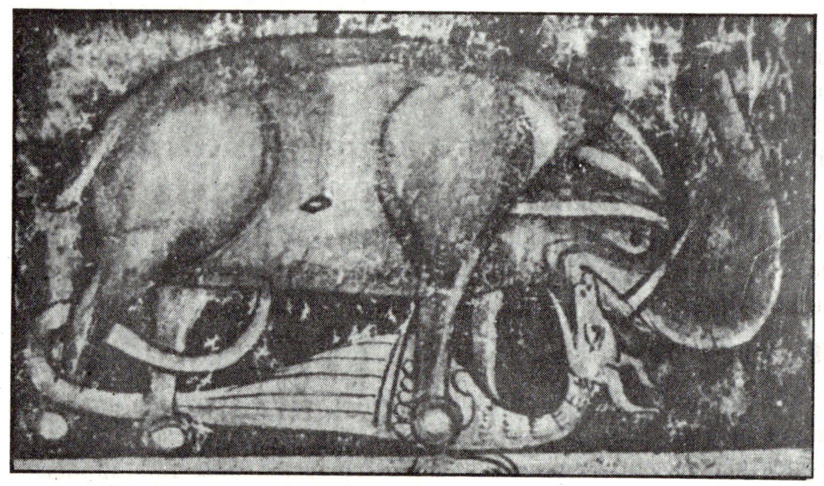

The elephant fighting with the dragon the former representing Adam and the latter the anti-Christ.

believed in the existence of dragons. In their maps they made the dragons so as to appear a reality. Perhaps they used it as a symbol for unknown land which was beyond their purview.

Some keen observers suggest that snakes, particularly boa constrictor or the python have dragonish qualities as they can enlarge up to 25 feet. In 1978, when a python had nearly swallowed a man in India, the villagers thought it to be a dragon. Although the villagers attacked only the python, but the victim also died with it.

While in some of the Indo-Malayan regions the flying lizards are often called by the name of 'Draco'. And an extraordinarily large lizard is called Komodo dragon. This lizard unlike the Draco, can expand up to 12 feet and has a long scaly body, an ugly head and forelegs. But it cannot fly. The flying lizard, Draco, is only about 6 inches long and has none of the dragonish qualities. Despite their meek resemblance, Dracos have helped to keep the dragon myth alive.

There are physical similarities among crocodiles, snakes, lizards, alligators and the dragons, as they all are reptiles. But such a resemblance is not enough to justify their becoming the source of the dragon legend. It is extremely difficult to trace out the source of the dragon myth.

Some researchers say that the source of dragon lies in the 'cosmic upheaval'. According to them when the orbit of Venus came close to the earth and devastation occurred, man looked at the stars and astronomy for help. This belief gave birth to various myths of the Aztecs, the Assyrians and the Babylonians. They supposed the Venus to be 'a feathered serpent', 'the fearful dragon', who nearly destroyed the earth.

According to them the dragon symbolises chaos and destruction. Nobody has been able to explain till today the connection that it has with the actual events. But people all over the world believe in it and usually attribute the unexplainable happenings of the world to dragons.

The Dragon Myth

Sir Grafton Elliott Smith collected dragon myths of the world. He came to the conclusion that dragon controls the rivers and seas and resides in wells or in clouds and is often responsible for thunder.

A late 18th century piece of furniture from Vietnam, showing two dragons chasing a pearl. It shows the interlocking of the negative feminine and the positive masculine forces in life.

lightening and other havocs caused by Nature. In short, the dragon controls the powers of the earth.

The art of the earlier days also represented dragons. The olden days artists made the dragons in the shape of the coiled or resting animals, somewhat in the form of a giant snake. Even the art, architecture and furniture of the olden days represented dragons as giant serpents.

The mythologies of different countries also represent the dragon myth. Some of the countries still support the idea that the earth rests on dragon's head. The natural disasters occur when the dragon turns its head. The Egyptians believe that their Sun God "RA" is surrounded by the coils of the serpent called Mehen. The Eastern Dragon is very different from the Western Dragon. The dragon of the East is a very beneficent animal. It became an emblem of power and the emperor of China sat on a dragon throne. He also put on 'dragon robes'.

The dragon image mirrors human obsessions through thousands of years. So all that can be said is that the dragon is not only very old, but it is also very strong. Hence the dragon myth also survives with full force. ■

Will The Egyptian Lands Disappear?

The growth of the Egyptian lands into a magnificent civilization is itself a mystery. Its splendid pyramids, giant sphinxes and statues, all are wonders for a modern man. Yet all does not seem to be well. The modern science with all its detailed and intensive research suggests that by 2100 A.D. major floods will swallow the great Egyption lands. How.........?

A wanderer into the Egyptian lands is struck with awe and wonder by the grandeur of the environment. The massive structures completely baffle the tourists. And one is forced to question: How did Egyptians build such beautiful giant structures and how did civilization blossom in this part of the land?

Let us have a look at another photograph of the Step Pyramid of King Zoser, which was built in or about 2650 B.C.

In the beginning this pyramid was in the form of a tomb having only

The Pyramids at Giza. They brood over the Egyptian landscape! It is hard to believe that these massive structures are just the tombs of kings.

Let us have a look at another photograph of the Step Pyramid of King Zoser, which was built in or about 2650 B.C.

one storey. It had a burial chamber beneath. Subsequently the builders started extending it and added three more layers to it. Thus it became a four step pyramid. But they were not satisfied with this extension. They finally added two more steps after further extending its base. These last two steps represent the dead king's passage to heaven.

Africa, during the Neolithic age, had become very inhabitable. There occurred a gradual decay of the flora and fauna. The soil also dried up. Because of the changes in the climate and ecology, people were forced towards the banks of the Nile, as these changes had not affected the Nile valley. Gradually this peaceful valley became full of the hustle and bustle of people. The fertile soil guaranteed food and shelter to all the inhabitants.

However, everything did not remain so peaceful. So the annual flooding occurred in the river and it inundated the wide strips of land on either side. But the water being rich in organic substances, created very fertile deposits of mud. No doubt the floods left behind a devastating environment. Often some of the villages and fields were swept away. Seeing all this the Neolithic Egypt started domesticating the river in place of animals or plants.

They built dykes and canals and taking help of the 'Shaduf', they could transfer water into canals. In this way the area used for cultivation was extended and civilization matured.

However, nowhere has nature been as baneful as in Egypt. Recently, Daniel J. Stanley, Senior Oceanographer at the Smithsoniah's National Museum of Natural History, declared that by the year 2100, there will be major flooding of vast areas of the Nile delta between Port Said on the Suez Canal in the east and the Damietta branch of the Nile in the West. According to Stanley the Mediterranean sea is cutting the shore line, which is subsequently regressing at the rate of 15 to 30 metres a year. And as the sea is acting like a saw, it is grinding away the soil and sediments in the area.

Explaining the behaviour of the sea, Stanley said that the gradual invasion of the sea is due to the rising level of the sea and the sinking level of the ground and the Azwan Dam on the Nile river.

So from Neolithic period to the modern 20th century, Egyptian lands have indeed undergone a lot of changes. Now, according to a Smithsonian researcher, these very mystique places, where more than a million people live, may disappear beneath the Mediterranean sea over the next century, as salt water rises and ground sinks in the north-eastern Nile river delta.

If Stanleys calculations become a reality, nothing will remain except a mystery for future generations to fathom. But when all is said and done the fact remains that the pyramids possess very great power to benefit mankind. Those who have examined the power of pyramids in a number of situations, point out that within a pyramid, "dry cell batteries regenerate; water seems tastier; food keeps longer; seeds germinate faster; pets and houseplants are happier; crystals grow in unusual forms; children appear calmer; sleep is better; menstrual cramps diminish; meditation is more concentrated; mental acuity improves; the sex drive increases; dowsers using a pendulum, dowsing rods or a forked twig can sense the force field of the pyramid; natural healing processes may be aided; prayer becomes more effective; and all psychic phenomena are stronger." Again Bill Kerrell and Kathy Groggin, in their book entitled 'The Guide to Pyramid Energy' (published in 1975), aptly remark, "Leave a cup of coffee under the pyramid for about twenty minutes. You'll find that the bitterness disappears and the flavour becomes mellower. Again this would seem to a lowering of the acidity level;......"

■

The Voice of Intuition

In 1971 Herbert Raiffe, a manufacturer of toys had an intuition that toy pandas were going to be much in demand in the very near future. He listened carefully to the voice of intuition and immediately acted upon the advice. He ordered the officers concerned of his factory that toy pandas be produced in large numbers. When President Nixon went to China and came back with a gift of two toy pandas, the demand for these toys increased all of a sudden. But it was no problem for Raiffe. He was fully prepared to meet the rapid increase in demand for the pandas. Consequently, his factory earned very large profits.

What is then the Voice of Intuition? Where does it come from? And how does it work? These are some of the questions which arise in our mind, when we think of the hidden voice.

In order to understand the Voice of Intuition, let us consider the following examples: (1) An educated poor man, Thomas, was without a job. He had a loving wife and a son. One fine evening his wife had felt in a flash that the problems of the family could be solved, if her husband went to see one of his very close friends. So she advised her husband accordingly. Thomas obeyed her and set out the next morning to meet his friend. While he boarded the train, a Voice spoke to him that he was soon going to have a solution to his problems. He felt very much encouraged and was full of enthusiasm and joy. When he reached his friend, he found that another gentleman had also come to see him from the neighbourhood. This gentleman was in need of an assistant in his office and the qualifications possessed by Thomas amply met his requirements. It was a wonderful experience. Thomas was offered the job, which he very gladly accepted. When he returned to his home, his wife was very much happy to learn that their economic difficulties were soon going to end. Here the Voice has acted twice. First in prompting his wife to advise Thomas to go to see his friend and secondly the Voice spoke to Thomas that soon he was going to have a solution to his problems. On both the occasions, the Voice aimed at the good of the family of Thomas.

(2) A young girl, Dorothy, was sent by her mother to bring a parcel from one of her relations. She started at about nightfall and had hardly gone half the distance, when she felt an urge to return her home. She immediately followed the advice and started returning her home. When she reached her home, she learnt that she was very badly required at home at that particular hour. She obeyed the directions of her inner voice, and was available at home in the hour of need. Thus the impending trouble was averted.

(3) One winter evening a young man, Jacob, had to go on an urgent assignment to meet one of his colleagues. There were two routes to carry him to the residence of his colleague. He felt a strong urge to go to that place by the longer route, avoiding the shorter one. He listened to the Voice and obeyed it. It was a dark night and just after going a few yards on the longer route, he kicked something lying on the ground. He picked it up and to his surprise he saw it in the street light and found that it was a purse containing twenty pound-notes. Jacob reported the matter immediately to the police and deposited the purse with them. The police waited for the owner for three months, but when no one turned up, the purse was returned to Jacob and he was told by the police that he could make use of the money that he had found that night.

Jacob was astounded. His wife had been ailing since long and the doctor had advised her a change of climate. Now he told his wife that he could take up a residence by the seaside and keep his wife there till she recovered fully. By obeying the inner Voice and going by the longer route that night he could benefit his family and afford proper treatment to his wife.

If you analyze the three instances cited above, you will find that there is a Voice of Intuition which exists in almost all of us and commands us in highly eloquent terms to adopt a particular course of action, which ultimately turns out to be in our interest. This is the Voice of Intuition for which no logical reasoning can be advanced. No rational explanation can be advanced for such incidents, for they are obviously beyond the realm of scientific experimentation.

The Voice of Intuition is the Voice of Wisdom itself. It is present in almost all the human beings and there is just a difference of degree. The Voice of Intuition is within you also and it is up to you to listen to its directions or disobey it. If you will disobey the Voice it will cease to guide you. Intuition becomes weaker, when you do not pay proper heed to its Voice. The Voice of Intuition seeks only the best for you and aims at your total well-being.

The Voice of Intuition belongs to the realm of extra-sensory perception. We will use the expression ESP for this to denote the realm of human thought beyond the field of sense organs and reason. This is the super-sensuous realm and reason is not applicable to it. ESP enables us to predict the future and to afford guidance to solve the problems which confront us. It is useful in almost every walk of life, be it business, politics, statesmanship or any other field of activities. When we follow the guidance of the ESP, it tends to grow and to make us better and stronger persons in our own field. The lawyers and the doctors are equally governed by the guidance that they receive from their power of ESP.

Dr. Douglas Dean interviewed a number of top businessmen such as William C. Durant, the founder of General Motors, Conrad Hilton, international hotel magnate, Chestor Carlson, the inventor of the photo copying technique, Kemmons Wilson, Chairman of Holiday Inns and a few others. He came to the conclusion that,..................ESP is an essential

Chestor Carlson, who invented the Xerox photocopying technique, was guided by his strong ESP and believed in the existence of similar psychic phenomena.

Charles Kemmons Wilson, founder and chairman of Holiday Inns Inc. He was guided by his very strong ESP in choosing a site for his hotel.

ingredient in business life where decisions have to be made about future events, often without enough information to justify them. Businessmen use it every week, evey month, every year, continually ....They pile up tremendous profits yearly because they really are stupendous at this ability."

Charles Kemmons Wilson, Chairman of Holiday Inns, Inc. was entrusted with the task of choosing the right site for his hotels. It is said about him that on certain occasions he would reject many sites by saying that they gave out a foul smell. Wilson could smell the site and decide. As soon as a site gave out a pleasant smell or fragrance, he would immediately say 'yes' to it. His strong ESP guided him in this regard.

Now we come to the politicians and statesmen. Abraham Lincoln, Winston Churchill, Franklin Roosevelt, Dr. S. Radhakrishnan and a few others, were all guided by their very strong ESP and followed the commands of their Intuition. They listened to their Voice of Intuition and were able to take decisions of very great significance, involving the destinies of millions of the citizens of their country. We will just mention about the abolition of slavery which is attributed to Abraham Lincoln. A very young lady, Nettie Colburn Maynard, was very close to President Lincoln, and while in trance, is reported to have laid very great emphasis on the necessity of the abolition of slavery. Here Lincoln's Voice of Intuition coupled with the message received through the young lady, Nettie, was the motivating force behind the historical decision taken by the President for the abolition of slavery.

Winston Churchill had invited three ministers to a dinner during the Second World War. While the dinner was going on, he had an 'intuition'. He immediately got up and went to the kitchen, where the butler and the maid were busy cooking the food. He instructed them to put the dinner on a hot-plate in the dining room and vacate the kitchen. It was observed that within less than five minutes, a bomb fell at the back of the house and the kitchen was totally destroyed. Every one was saved as they had time to go to the shelter. The dinner also concluded peacefully. It is just one instance of the Voice of Intuition obeyed by the great statesman. His intuitive powers helped him throughout his life and he had made it a point to obey the Voice without raising any question.

Franklin Roosevelt also had faith in the Voice of Intuition. On several occasions he obeyed the commands of his own Voice, but on certain other occasions, he also consulted a psychologist, Jeane Dixon, who was known as the Washington seer. Dixon's Voice of Intuition could offer very satisfactory guidance to Roosevelt.

Winston Churchill and Franklin Roosevelt

The Voice of Intuition is thus the innate wisdom and guidance which is available to all human beings at all times. Particularly when one is in some serious trouble and is full of anxiety, there is a flash and a direction given by the Voice itself. Such experiences are very many and if an individual obeys the Voice of Intuition he can make very great progress in his life. But the mystery remains, for it cannot be explained on the basis of scientific laws. As we have already seen a direction comes to us when we badly need it and we have just to reduce the command into action without letting any time elapse. If we allow the time to drift away, we will not be able to resolve our problems and shall be worse for not having obeyed the commands and guidance of the Voice of Intuition.

Benjamin Fairless, former Chairman of the Board of U.S. Steel said that while you obey your 'Intuition', "You do not know how you do it; you just do it." With regular practice, you will find that there is a very close relation between following the commands of Intuition and making profits in business and achieving the goal of one's life. ■

The Significance of Dreams : Do They Foretell?

Perhaps no other phenomena of mental life have aroused such a great curiosity and wonder as the 'dreams'. Men, women and children of all countries have ever shown a keen interest in the dreams that they have seen. They want to know the meaning of their dreams and go to those who excel in the art of interpretation of dreams. A mystery is always woven around the dreams and it requires a keen insight and vast experience to tell a man the significance of his dream.

We are told that Lakshman Singh, the Maharana of Chittore, was commanded by the goddess whom he worshipped, that he should not delay in starting a campaign against Aurangzeb, the fanatic Moghul king. This command was given to the Maharana in a dream. In the same strain, we read that Akbar, the Great, had asked Jahangir in a dream to pardon one of his courtiers, who had committed a heinous crime.

There is a great mystery surrounding the phenomena of dreams. We will try to explain to what extent such phenomena can be explained scientifically. And where no scientific explanation is possible, we will have to rest content with the mystery of the matter and wait for the time, when it will be unravelled.

Dreams differ from the conscious mental activities of a living being in allowing a free play to our imagination. Thus they share in the characteristics of life-play where freedom and spontaneity are present. Dreams are mainly of two kinds, first the day-dreams and second the night dreams. The former are experienced in actual waking life of a person, while the latter come to us while we are in bed asleep. Day-dreams are very common with children, particularly during the period of adolescence, when there is a lack of enough practical sense in them. Sometimes daydreaming adopts a serious form, when an adolescent loses all touch with the material world, and prefers to dwell in the realm of phantasy alone. Daydreams are mainly of three kinds, first of all there are pleasant daydreams, which are of a very agreeable nature, the second are the mastery daydreams and the third are the anxiety day dreams which give rise to worrying. The second form of daydreams allow the subject to satisfy his or her craving for leadership and self-display which so much dominates a young mind. The third type of daydreams characterise those subjects who are given to worry and anxiety without there being any legitimate cause for the same. It gives rise to a brooding disposition.

Night-dreams, which are usually described as 'dreams' are "play of imagination, even freer from control and criticism than the daydream." We may refer to no less than three essential features of such dreams. Firstly, the images and senses are presented in a very incoherent form. Hardly there is any order in them and contradictions are not very uncommon. We may see a parrot turning into a crow or a human being changing into an animal or a bird. Secondly, the scenes and pictures visible during sleep are accepted to be *real* as long as the dream continues. Thirdly, the dreams are often presented in a mask or a disguise. The actual objects of daily experience assume a disguised form and become symbols for something else.

Now a very pertinent question arises: Why do we dream? What are the factors which are responsible for dreams? To answer these questions, we will refer to the theory of dreams as expounded by a well-known psychologist and hypnotist, Dr Sigmund Freud. He tells us that our dreams fulfil the motives, wishes and desires which cannot be satisfied in the actual conditions of our waking life. We aspire for many objects and often 'pine for what is not', but the rigidities of decorum, customs, traditons, convention and civilization make it highly difficult for us to give vent to our feelings and emotions. The consequences are not too far difficult to anticipate, for the wishes, desires, feelings and emotions are very powerful and cannot be imprisoned in a closed cabin. More often than not, these motivating forces reveal themselves in our sleep and dreams when the 'censor' is not active and the sanctions of morality are silent and do not interfere with their realization. Let us cite certain examples in support of Freud's theory. "An adult frequently dreams of finding money, first a copper in the dust, and then silver close by, and then more and more, till he wakes up and spoils it all........." Similar instances are found in "the sex dreams of sexually abstinent persons, or the polar explorers' recurring dream of warm, green fields." The wish-fulfilling character of dreams has also assumed a proverbial nature. Some of these are, "The pig dreams of acorns and the goose of maize." And also, "What do chickens dream of?" The answer is "of millet'."

While the chief factor responsible for dreams is the non-fulfilment of a desire or a wish in conscious waking experience, it must be carefully noted that the suppressed desire or wish does not always receive its fulfilment in exactly the same form in which it is entertained. The reason is that there is a mental policeman that checks the suppressed desires from being fulfilled in the same form. Freud calls this policeman a 'censor' which controls our desires in waking life. But when we are asleep, the censor, too, becomes inactive and the unfulfilled desires seek their gratification *symbolically*. The desire or wish that seeks gratification in dreams often puts on a mask and its original nature has to be analyzed carefully.

Let us take for example the dream of flying. Most of us will recall their own experiences when they saw that they were flying in the air with the ease of the feathered people. But the dream symbolises some other deeper meaning diferent from its manifest content. The dream symbolises the achievement or target in a quick and pleasant manner. This may be called its latent content and affords strength to a human being to strive to achieve one's goal. The latent content (the term used by Freud to signify the suggested meaning of a dream) signifies that the dreamer, if and when in difficulty, has always desired to reach his goal in a pleasant and easy manner. He has ever desired to avoid hardships and difficulties without having been made to traverse the thorny path, so that he is anxious to pass only through the bed of roses. It is a fact that most of us pursue only the lead of pleasure and avoid the lead of pain. Our actions are generally performed in the line of least resistance and the difficult path is normally avoided.

The standpoint of Freud may appear to be quite strange to many a mind. Even commonsense seems to lend its support to his views on symbolism. Even the layman thinks that if he dreams of a mountain, it stands for a serious problem or difficulty. Poetry, drama, folk-lores and myths often contain a thickly woven network of symbols. Dancing, one of the most beautiful of all arts, is symbolical in its highest manifestations. No wonder that our dreams are also an expression of the same phenomena. Symbolism has rendered a fairly satisfactory hypothesis in the hands of the psycho-analysts in understanding the abnormal mental conditions of their subjects.

Do Dreams Foretell?

There are no doubt certain dreams that reveal the gratification of repressed desires, but all our dreams are not of this category. Freud's theory of dreams helps us to understand quite a good number of our dreams, but not all of them. There are other dreams which contain premonitions. They predict the future and warn us against happenings which may not be to our advantage.

Charles Dickens, the famous novelist, describes one of his dreams in the following lines:

"I dreamed that I saw a lady in a red shawl with her back towards me............On her turning round, I found that I didn't know her and she said, 'I am Miss Napier'.

"All the time I was dressing next morning, I thought—what a preposterous thing to have so very distinct a dream about nothing ! and why Miss Napier. That same Friday night I read. After the reading, came into my retiring room Miss Boyle and her brother, and *the* lady in the red shawl whom they present as 'Miss Napier'!"

Here the dream told Dickens of a future happening. We also give below two dreams which had predicted the future and the premonitions contained in them were borne out by future happenings. A British engineer, John W. Dunne, explained the precognition in dreams in his

John W. Dunne, a British aeronautical engineer, who had a vivid dream of a serious train accident. His dream predicted the accident and some of the details revealed in dream were absolutely true.

The Archduke Ferdinand, just before his assassination by Serbian nationalists.

book entitled 'An Experiment With Time' published in 1927. He describes one of his dreams in the following words:

Dunne tried to recollect the date of the accident, but all that he could recollect was that it was going to occur some time in the coming spring. And on April 14, 1914, the unfortunate accident took place, when a mail train 'Flying Scotsman' jumped the parapet near Burntisland station, 15 miles *north of the Forth Bridge?* and fell down 20 feet below.

Let us mention another dream seen by a Balkan Bishop, Monseigneur Joseph de Lanvi, in the night of June 27, 1914. The Bishop had received a letter in his dream, which secretly portrayed a street on which a car was moving. The Archduke Ferdinand was seated in the car with his wife facing a general. Another officer was also seated in the car beside the driver. Suddenly the two officers came forward and fired at the 'royal couple'. The letter of the Archduke Ferdinand read as follows: 'Your Eminence, dear Dr. Lanyi, my wife and I have been victims of a political crime at Sarajevo. We commend ourselves to your prayers. Sarajevo, 28 June 1914, 4 a.m.'

The very next day, the Bishop received the news of the assassination of the Archduke Ferdinand. Within a few weeks, the First World War commenced.

Thus we may conclude by saying that the phenomena of dreams are very difficult to be correctly interpreted. While most of the dreams fulfil our repressed desires, there are a few dreams that predict our future as well. Future events are sometimes visible in our dreams. Hence we can say that dreams also predict the future. Still there is much in the phenomena of dreams that eludes scientific understanding. ■

The Mysterious Unconscious

One of the most significant contributions of Modern Psychology is its emphasis on the 'unconscious mental processes'. The 'unconscious' owes its development to the researches carried on by the school of Contemporary Psychology known as Psycho-Analysis. The main thing remarkable about this school is that it has grown out of medicine. The chief exponents of this school are Freud, Adler and Jung. These eminent persons have been busy in finding out details about the mysterious ways in which the 'unconscious' functions.

The exponents of Depth Psychology have compared our mind to the tip of an ice-berg floating on the surface of water. A large part of the iceberg is under the level of water and only a small portion of it is visible to the naked eye. The portion of the iceberg which is visible to us is just 1/8 of the entire body of ice. Hence 7/8 part thereof is submerged and cannot be seen.

Thus our mind has been divided into two zones: one the 'conscious' and the other 'the unconscious'. The conscious mental processes comprise our behaviour during waking life and consist of activities such as perceiving, attending, observing, remembering, imagining, reasoning and thinking. The major portion of our mind thus consists of the unconscious mental processes, which we cannot know directly.

The 'unconscious' plays a vital role in human life. It is visible in the common errors which we often commit, e.g., forgetting one's handkerchief at a friend's place, holding a pen in one's own hand and still looking for it, or standing in the corner and placing one's walking stick on the bed in a posture of sleep. Similarly there are slips of pen and slips of tongue, too many to be accounted for. A man wants to pronounce the word 'wish' and speaks out 'fish'. So there are many slips of pen when we write a word wrongly, not because we do not know the spelling, but because the wrong spelling comes out involuntarily. Cases have been observed when

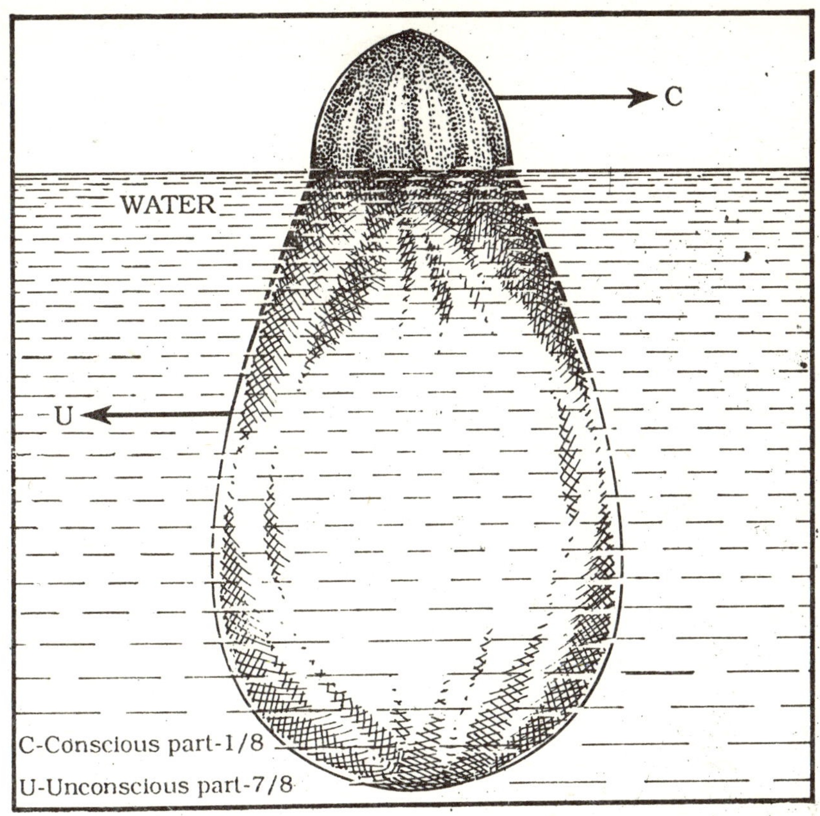

An iceberg floating on the surface of water represents the mind as a whole. The portion of the iceberg which is visible represents the conscious mental processes, while that which is underwater indicates the unconscious mind.

writing a letter to our near and dear we just address, "My dear dear ....." There are numerous such examples.

The most important evidence for the existence of the 'unconscious' is found in sleep, when it is most active. Often we have observed that when we are facing a difficult problem in mathematics or physics and we go to sleep with it, we get up early next morning with a suggested solution to our problem. We often come across hard and difficult problems in our personal and social life and fail to find its solution. Often a suggestion to solve the difficult situation comes to us when we sleep over it. And when we get up next morning, we find that there is a very helpful suggestion in our mind for resolving the difficult situation. Thus during sleep the

August Kekule, the gifted German scientist, discovered the structure of benzene.

conscious mental processes do not function, but the 'unconscious' gets the fullest opportunity to function.

Sleep and dreams usually go together. We have read about dreams in the preceding chapter, but here we are going to learn about a dream of a scientist, whose 'unconscious' helped him to discover the structure of benzene. The name of the scientist who had the dream of discovery is August Kekule. He wanted to work out the manner in which the hydrogen and carbon atoms were linked together in benzene. The solution came to him one day when he was half asleep, a conditon mid way between waking and sleeping. He saw the benzene molecule in the form of a snake rolled into a circle. Kekule got up and guessed that the problem could be solved if the six 'carbon atoms formed a ring, with the hydrogen atoms attached. An enormous field, the chemistry of the ring compounds, was

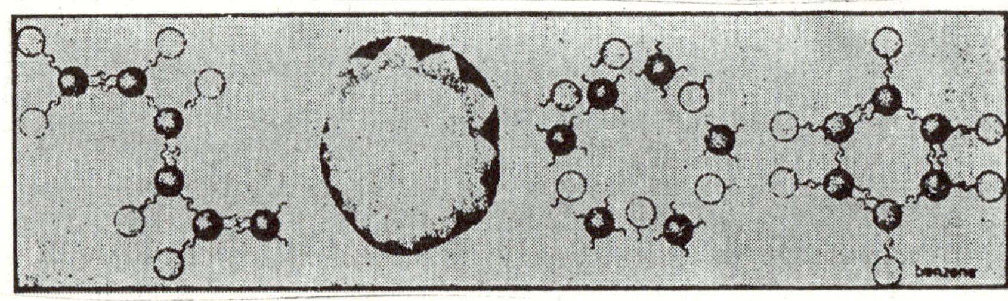

Benzene in which the hydrogen and carbon atoms were linked together.

Samuel Taylor Coleridge dreamed his poem "Kubla Khan" and reduced his dream on paper the very next morning. The unconscious provided him the inspiration and the scenes were visible in dreams.

opened up, and became the basis of the prosperous German dye industry.*

There are several other cases of eminent poets, thinkers and artists who have been guided by their dreams and have given their best to the world. Johann Wolfgang von Goethe, the great German poet, scientist and philosopher not ony solved many problems while he was asleep, but he also composed many poems which related to the inspirations that he had received in his dreams. It is reported that Samuel Taylor Coleridge composed his reputed poem, *Kubla Khan,* in his dream. Here the role of the 'unconscious' is very clearly visible.

We will now discuss the 'unconscious' as it has been viewed by Dr Sigmund Freud, pioneer in the field of Psycho-Analysis. He offers us the concept of 'repression' to account for the 'unconscious'. There are several desires that we experience which cannot be satisfied in our waking life. These desires go down to the realm of the 'unconscious' and reside there. Most of the desires that go to the unconscious realm are mostly anti-social and our society does not permit their frank expression and realization. Freud uses a very interesting analogy of a house having two storeys. The residents of the first floor are respectable persons, while those who live on the ground floor are those who are unable to conform to the standards of civilization and etiquette. Our conscious mind represents the civilized people who are living on the first floor, while the 'unconscious' resembles the people who are living on the ground floor. In other words, the conscious mind is usually well adjusted and functions in harmony with the code of conduct laid down by the society. On the contrary, the unconscious mind contains all those unfulfilled desires which we cannot fulfil due to social laws and customs.

According to Freud the 'repressed' desires are generally sexual in nature. He no doubt uses the term *sex* in a very wide sense so as to include within its purview all that is connected with the feelings of affection and the sentiment of love. So much so that he traces the earliest beginnings of this motive in the thumb sucking activity of the small infant. The repressed desires are sexual in nature and are highly powerful motives functioning during sleep and dreams.

Sometimes it may also happen that our 'repressed' desires do not find an opportunity to come to the forefront and may remain in the 'unconscious' for a number of years. The conscious and rational self of a man does not permit him to satisfy his desire due to social laws, and the desires persist and remain in the 'unconscious'. Generally a man rationalises his desires and satisfies them in a manner permissible by society. But in circumstances where this is not possible, the repressed desire assumes the form of a mental conflict resulting in the experience of tension by the individual. Mental conflict gives rise to several mental troubles ranging from anxiety, worry and mania to certain others forms of serious psychoses and neuroses. For the treatment of such mental diseases, we have to go to a psychiatrist, who makes an attempt to diagnose our trouble. Freud also suggested that the present trouble is to be traced back to its origin and in many cases the roots of the present trouble will be found to lie in the infancy of the patient. When we shall study the infancy of the patient, we will certainly find many such desires which could not be satisfied due to the social laws and the sanctions of morality.

In order to understand the roots of the present mental trouble, Freud has sugested the technique of 'free association' for understanding the patient correctly. The 'free association' technique requires that the patient will be allowed full liberty to speak out what-so-ever comes into his head. Usually there is a tendency to suppress one's thoughts, feelings and emotions but by careful handling the resistance may be controlled. If the psychiatrist established a rapport with the patient, he will give out almost all that is hidden within him. Consequently the diagnosis will be facilitated.

The 'unconscious' thus is a very mysterious part of human mind.

The ideas, thoughts, feelings and emotions that it contains govern our behaviour. Our 'unconscious' has been at times of very great help to us and has been responsible for many discoveries in the field of science, mathematics and philosophy. The 'unconscious' has also to be studied as a repository of our 'repressed desires' and unfulfilled wishes, which has been the main field of study for the psycho-analysts. Gradually the unfathomable mysteries of the 'unconscious' will reveal themselves to us more and more. ■

The Ghosts

The ghosts belong to the world of apparitions and are visible in certain peculiar and bizarre situations. It is very difficult to understand them and the causes which are responsible for their occurrence are not easy to grasp.

The phenomena of ghosts have interested man since ages past. But now we have begun to find out scientific reasons for their existence. Some of the parapsychologists are busy in analysing them by using scientific techniques.

We will try to ascertain the mystery underlying ghosts and will refer to a few experiences of ghosts by some of the psychical researchers.

The ghosts are visible in the form of apparitions devoid of human characteristics. Their sights are airy and cannot be touched by our hands. The ghost of the person is etherial. It can be seen and also heard if the arrival of the ghost is accompanied by certain sounds or meaningful remarks.

First of all we will cite the ghost of Reverend Dr Harris, who used to visit Athenaeum Library after his death. The ghost of Dr Harris was regularly seen by the famous American Novelist, Hawthorne, when he too visited the Library for study and research. He found Dr Harris sitting in the chair, where he used to sit during his life time and study the *Boston Post,* the paper which was very dear to Dr Harris during his visits to the Library. Hawthorne did not know in the beginning that Dr. Harris was not alive and treated the ghost of Dr Harris as the actual person. When one of the friends of Hawthorne told him that he had passed away, he was very much surprised. His curiosity increased day by day and he saw that no one who recognised Dr Harris ever talked to him. Of course, the rules of the Library did not permit any talk between one person and another, but even when they came out of the Library, there was no conversation

Nathaniel Hawthorne (1804-1864)
He has given a very clear account of the ghost of Dr. Harris, to an extent that it forms a first class evidence in support of the ghost.

between the apparition and other persons, who were his very close friends, during the lifetime of Dr Harris.

There is another very interesting example of the ghost of a *man in grey*. The ghost was seen throughout the time of Queen Anne and the Victorian era and also during the twentieth century between 1930 and 1960. The historian and theatre critic, W.J. McQueen Pope, saw the ghost several times, and made efforts to find out the identity of the person whose ghost was visible in 'grey'. All that could be concluded was that it was the ghost of some actor who was dressed in 'grey' for a particular scene. The ghost was visible in the hall of Theatre Royal in Drury Lane, London, for over 200 years. The very close association of the actor with the theatre can very well be concluded reasonably. Very often it so happens that if and when we are very much attached to a particular person, place or thing, during our life time, our spirit or soul visits that person or place or remains close to the object even after the death of our body. It is a self-established principle that our soul never dies. Only the body dies, when the life is gone out of it. It is true that no one knows where the soul goes or how does it live, but the immortality of the soul is a fundamental principle of all religions and morality. The ghost or apparition is just a vision of the immortal soul coming close to the person, place or thing which was very closely associated with it during the period of its being *embodied* its. It would be befitting to distinguish a ghost from a hallucination. When we perceive an object without there being an outside stimulus, it is called 'hallucination". It represents more or less an abnormal mental condition of the subject which is surcharged with the intensity of feelings and emotions. There may be just one dominating

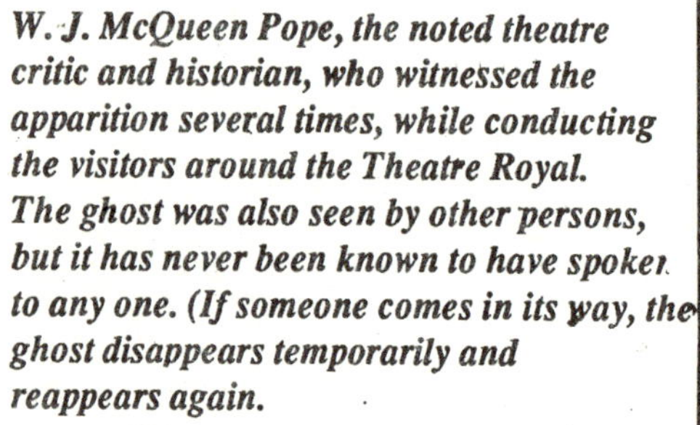

W. J. McQueen Pope, the noted theatre critic and historian, who witnessed the apparition several times, while conducting the visitors around the Theatre Royal. The ghost was also seen by other persons, but it has never been known to have spoken to any one. (If someone comes in its way, the ghost disappears temporarily and reappears again.

emotion such as 'fear', 'anger' or 'love' or more than one emotion may be combined with each other, at a time, and give rise to a hallucination. A nervous housewife often wakes up when she hears the sound of burglars moving from room to room along the corridor. In Shakespeare's drama, "The Macbeth", Macbeth visualises the blood stained dagger so very clearly that it takes the form of a hallucination and strikes him with terror.

On the contrary when we observe an apparition or a ghost, there is something objective that we see, it can be seen by others also and may be repeated a number of times without our wanting to see it. The hallucination is purely subjective and cannot be observed by other persons sitting close to the subject. Hence we should not confuse a ghost with a hallucination and try to understand both the phenomena separately and distinct from the other.

We close our treatment of ghosts with the following quotation, "The perennial question as to whether ghosts exist must, in view of various surveys carried out by such bodies as the British Society for Psychical Research (SPR) over the last 100 years or so, be answered in the affirmative. To reject the testimony of the many hundreds of respectable people who claim to have experienced apparitions as wishful thinking, self-delusion or downright lying would be sheer wilfulness." ■

Do You Speak to Your Plants?

Do you speak to your plants? The question may appear to you to be very peculiar, for how can you talk to a plant and how can a plant understand your language? Hence on the very face of it you will be inclined to reply to this question in the negative.

But in many cases the reality differs from what it appears to us. The size of the sun and the moon differs from that which we perceive with our naked eye. When you travel in the railway train, you find that the trees, the houses and other objects are moving behind. You endow them with the capacity of movement, though actually the trees and the houses remain in their own positions and it is actually the train that has speeded forward.

A recent school of botanists has arisen which believes that the plant can perform conscious activities and it can feel and reason and can direct its activity. Hence you can speak to your plants and rest assured that they would respond to your words.

The Indian traditions are full of instances when trees and plants are worshipped by human beings. Let us take the case of a banyan tree and a holy basil plant. There is a particular day in the month of June when the married women worship the banyan tree and pray for the long life of their husbands. The women dress themselves nicely, keep a fast and go to the banyan tree and speak to it in the following words, "My dear respected banyan tree, protect my husband from all dangers and grant him a very long life of happiness and prosperity." In case there be any other requirement of the lady the same is also spoken of to the tree. And it is firmly believed that the tree listens to the words of the lady who prays and responds to the same. Similar is the case with the holy basil plant. It is worshipped almost daily by the devotees and the request is made in prayer for protection of the family in the time of difficulty. The prayer is addresed to the plant and the plant responds. These examples just go to prove the hypothesis that plants and trees are sensitive and conscious human speech and respond to it. The plants react to human emotions as well.

We will now refer to a few scientific investigations to prove that the plants have feelings and are really very sensitive to sound and vibrations. Luther Burbank of Santa Rosa, California, who was very much famous for his nurseries, experimented for a number of years to develop a variety of cactus without spines. He spoke to his plants very lovingly in the following words, "You have nothing to fear. You don't need your defensive thorns. I will protect you." And the plants responded to his words. They understood his speech. He told the plants that he held their lives in very great regard and affection. In the words of Manly P. Hall, the President of the Philosophical Research Society of Los Angeles, the love of the scientist, Burbank, provided a kind of subtle nourishment that made everything grow better and bear fruit more abundantly." Mr Burbank also propounded the theory that plants have more than twenty sensory perceptions.

The famous Indian scientist, Sir Jagdish Chandra Bose, professor

Luther Burbank, the eminent botanist, who succeeded in growing a spineless cactus. He believed that the plants could understand the meaning of his gentle and loving remarks.

of physics at Presidency College, Calcutta, also carried out his experiments on the '20 sensory perceptions of the plant' in 1900s. He found that the plants have no nervous system, but they respire and digest their food. And what was very strange was the fact that the plants could move without there being any muscles.

Thus the responses given out by plants resembled the responses of animals. There was a close resemblance between the skins of reptiles and amphibians on the one hand and the skins of plants of fruits and vegetables on the other. The plants also get tired of 'continuous stimulation' as do the animals. There was also a similarity between the responses of the leaves of plants to light and the eyes of the animals to the same stimulus. The plants could also be rendered 'unconscious' by the administration of chloroform as was the case with animals.

The findings of Luther Burbank and Sir Jagdish Chandra Bose were very much alike in so far as the nature of plant's '20 sensory' perceptions was concerned. Thus their researches have established beyond any shadow of doubt that the plants respond to stimuli much in the same manner as the animals do.

Now we shall briefly refer to the research carried on by a lady scientist, Dorothy Retallack, to find out the responses made by the plants to music. She performed her experiments in 1968 at Denver, Colorado. She took a mixed group of plants consisting of philodendron, corn, radishes, pelargoniums and African violets. The musical notes were played on the piano for twelve hours a day. After a period of three weeks, it was observed that all the plants which leaned away from the source of sound had died except the African violets. The plants which were in the control group and were not subjected to noise, had grown normally.

Dorothy Retallack arrived at the following conclusions as a result of her investigations:

(1) 'Rock music' affected the plants adversely. They developed a tendency to move away from the source of music and had an abnormal growth.

(2) Bach, Haydn and Indian 'sitar' music created positive effects on the plants and the plants had an accelerated growth.

(3) Folk-music had neutral effect on the growth of plants.

Before we come to an end of our discussion, it would be quite interesting to note that Mr. Pierre Paul Sauvin, an officer of the International telephone and Telegraph in New Jersey had a radio transmitter attached to his leg under the trousers. Through this transmitter he would talk to his plants at home in a very affectionate and loving manner. His conversation would last for a few minutes and he would also listen to the responses received from his pet plants. It is just an example which illustrates the extent to which a man can go in taking care of the plants in his home. But we may come across thousands of people who go on talking to their plants while they are watering them or bathing their petals, and the result too is within their easy access: the plants grow at a faster speed and in a more beautiful form than others who are not conversant with it. The researches of many devoted scientists lead us to the inevitable conclusion that "talking in a friendly tone to any plant will result in its improved growth and health"

We have referred in the beginning to a recent school of scientists that believes that the plants possess feelings and can also reason. The chief exponents of this school are Francais in Germany, the academicians Famintsin and Borodin and particularly Professor Polovtsey in Russia. The theories propounded by these eminent scientists have a number of mysterious phenomena in Nature to support them.

Now that it is established that the plants are endowed with feelings and consciousness, we end with a question raised by a French newspaper la Matin: When we strike a woman with a blossom who suffers more the woman or the flower?" ■

POPULAR SCIENCE

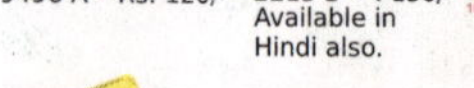

9496 A • Rs. 120/-

2215 S • ₹ 150/- Available in Hindi also. Contains 10 Projects

2214 S • ₹ 150/- Available in Hindi also.

Set Code: 4514 S

Set 4 Vols.: ₹ 780

Each Vol.: ₹ 195/

Available in Hindi & English both

8716 T • ₹ 160/-

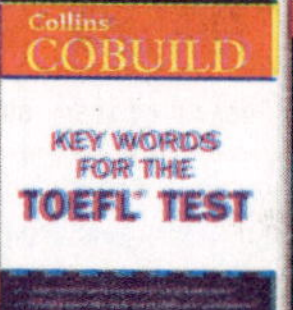

HC009 • ₹ 620/-

HC008 • ₹ 399/-

HC005 • ₹ 540/-

This Library is must for every student of a School or a College

Also equally useful for everyone else

Price: ₹ 600/-

Contains 4 books of ₹ 150/- each

8702 B • ₹ 150/-

6678 D • ₹ 195/-

6679 A • ₹ 150/-

9660 K • ₹ 250/-

4 Books of the Library

₹ 150/- Page 256 (with CD) English Conversation

₹ 150/- Page 310 Grammar & Punctuation

₹ 150/- Page 316 How to use English

₹ 150/- Page 344 English Vocabul

QUIZ BOOKS

8965 D • ₹ 150/-

7726 K • ₹ 120/-

7727 L • ₹ 120/-

7723 F • ₹ 100/-

9412 C • ₹ 120/-

7753 G • ₹ 100/-

7725 B • ₹ 100/-

7722 E • ₹ 100/-

GENERAL BOOKS

9532 D • ₹ 250/- HB

8526 B • ₹ 125/-

8712 M • ₹ 150/-

8711 K • ₹ 1

9821 K • ₹ 175/-

9699 T • ₹ 100/-

9767 B • ₹ 150/-

5114 B • ₹ 8

4175 A • ₹ 195/-

9459 H • ₹ 1000/- (HB)

9041 A • ₹ 195/-

4022 D • ₹ 1

SELF-IMPROVEMENT

New

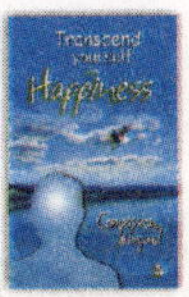

3 R • ₹ 195/- 9498 C • ₹ 180/- 9490 H • ₹ 175/- 9464 R • ₹ 80/- 9096 B • ₹ 120/- 5614 E • ₹ 150/- 4008 J • ₹ 120/- 9026 D • ₹ 120/- 9786 M • ₹ 195/-

1 J • ₹ 100/- 8885 D • ₹ 80/- 9081 D • ₹ 150/- 9091 B • ₹ 120/- 9060 B • ₹ 120/- 9684 F • ₹ 195/- 8928 D • ₹ 80/- 9449 A • ₹ 195/- 9788 R • ₹ 195/-

MANAGEMENT/JOB/CARRIER/BUSINESS & PROFESSION

All Time Bestsellers

61 K • ₹ 135/- 5338 A • ₹ 135/- with CD 8979 A • ₹ 120/- 9406 B • ₹ 150/- 5441 D • ₹ 195/- 8883 D • ₹ 120/- 9672 G • ₹ 150/- 9682 D • ₹ 120/-

New

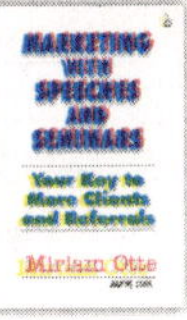

697 P • ₹ 195/- 9313 D • ₹ 150/- 5623 B • ₹ 195/- 9439 L • ₹ 150/- 4005 E • ₹ 150/- 5643 B • ₹ 120/- 9431 C • ₹ 175/- 8990 C • ₹ 96/-

18 D • ₹ 150/- 9079 B • ₹ 195/- 5618 D • ₹ 120/- 5640 C • ₹ 120/- 5615 D • ₹ 150/- 8972 C • ₹ 80/- 4001 A • ₹ 150/- 5646 A • ₹ 225/- 4017 D • ₹ 120/-

PERSONALITY DEVELOPMENT

9670 E • ₹ 240/- 9678 R • ₹ 195/- 9450 B • ₹ 195/- 9487 E • ₹ 150/- 9466 T • ₹ 96/- 5639 B • ₹ 80/- 5641 A • ₹ 150/- 9088 C • ₹ 1

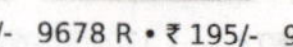

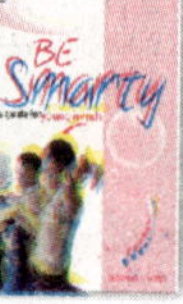

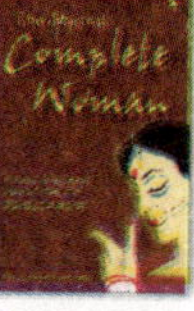

9667 B • ₹ 150/- 9666 A • ₹ 150/- 9696 M • ₹ 220/- 9973 B • ₹ 110/- 9981 B • ₹ 96/- 8868 D • ₹ 120/- 8966 E • ₹ 100/- 9070 B • ₹ 195/-9028 D • ₹ 1

STUDENT DEVELOPMENT

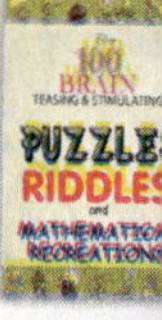

9090 A • ₹ 195/- 9668 C • ₹ 150/- 9071 D • ₹ 140/- 9455 C • ₹ 150/- 5622 A • ₹ 120/- 9967 C • ₹ 120/- 2241 J • ₹ 100/- 94441 S • ₹ 195/-9654 D • ₹ 10

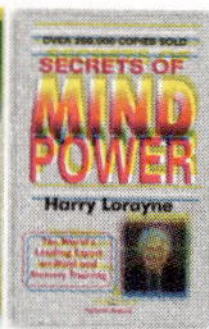

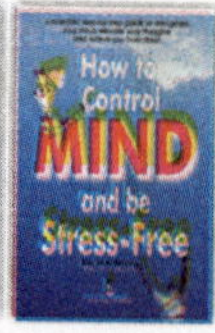

9652 D • ₹ 120/- 8962 A • ₹ 100/- 9089 D • ₹ 135/- 4016 D • ₹ 160/- 4009 K • ₹ 110/- 8997 B • ₹ 120/- 4010 L • ₹ 100/- 9787 P • ₹ 100/- 2244 D • ₹ 8

SAYING/QUOTATIONS/PROVERBS

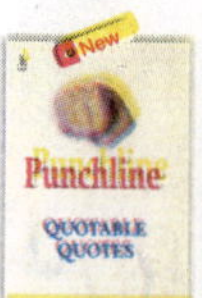

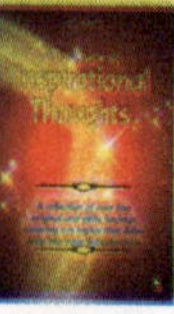

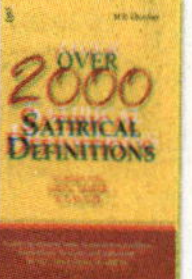

9474 F • ₹ 170/- 9789 A • ₹ 150/- 9953 A • ₹ 100/- 8947 E • ₹ 100/- 8999 D • ₹ 80/- 5512 A • ₹ 150/- 8963 B • ₹ 80/- 8890 D • ₹ 150/- 9925 A • ₹ 60

HINDOOLOGY / RELIGION / SPIRITUAL BOOKS

New

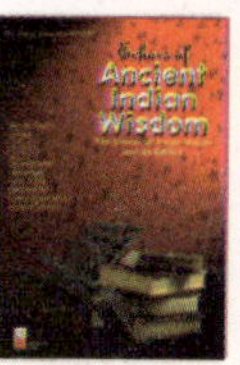

9873 C • ₹ 60/- | 9770 E • ₹ 150/- | 9799 D • ₹ 160/- | 9453 A • ₹ 195/- | 4179 A • ₹ 295/- (HB) | 4128 D • ₹ 295/- (HB) | 4138 B Rs. 250 (PB) | 4181 C • ₹ 19

4177 B • ₹ 195/- | 9997 C • ₹ 80/- | 4182 D • ₹ 96/- | 9984 E • ₹ 399/- (HB) | 4130 B • ₹ 120/- | 4183 A • ₹ 350/- (HB) | 4151 A • ₹ 399/-

9811 P • ₹ 120/- | 9585 A • ₹ 96/- | 9405 A • ₹ 195/- | 9989 D • ₹ 96/- | 9508 D • ₹ 95/- | 4134 B • ₹ 80/- | 4188 A • ₹ 1

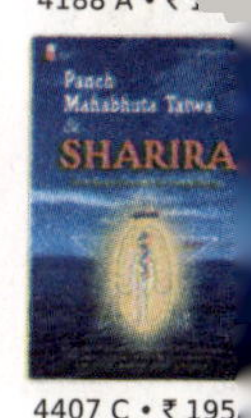

9504 D • ₹ 100/- | 4133 A • ₹ 60/- | 9513 A • ₹ 195/- | 4126 B • ₹ 96/- | 9812 R • ₹ 120/- | 4152 B • ₹ 96/- | 4407 C • ₹ 195/

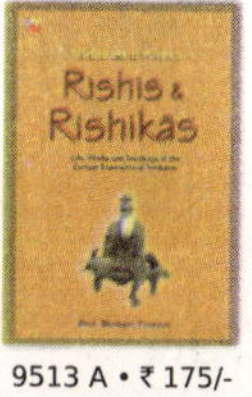

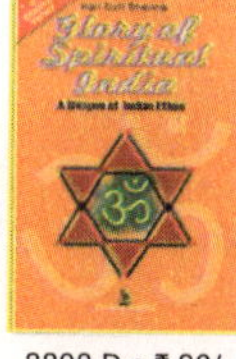

9504 D • ₹ 100/- | 4124 A • ₹ 120/- | 9513 A • ₹ 175/- | 9520 D • ₹ 120/- | 9987 E • ₹ 150/- | 8898 D • ₹ 80/- | 4190 C • ₹ 160/

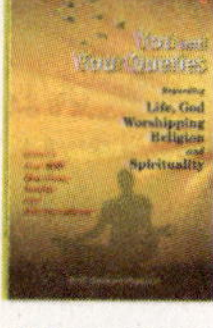

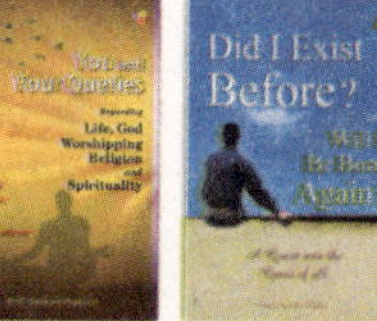

9509 A • ₹ 150/- | 9510 B • ₹ 120/- | 9525 A • ₹ 150/- | 9540 D • ₹ 150/- | 9542 B • ₹ 150/- | 9514 B • ₹ 60/- | 4132 D • ₹ 100/- | 9069 A • ₹ 80/-

ALTERNATIVE THERAPIES

32 F • ₹ 180/-

8983 E • ₹ 100/-

8836 D • ₹ 135/-

9935 F • ₹ 120/-

37 D • ₹ 96/-

8889 D • ₹ 80/-

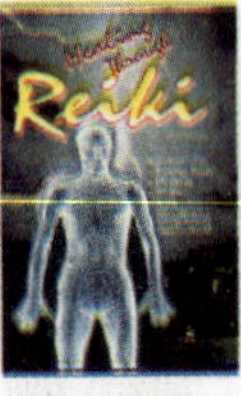

8842 D • ₹ 100/-

8941 A • ₹ 80/-

GENERAL HEALTH

9075 C • ₹ 225/-

8877 A • ₹ 120/-

9940 D • ₹ 150/-

8859 G • ₹ 80/-

9038 A • ₹ 68/-

8847 M • ₹ 100/-

8870 D • ₹ 100/-

9950 B • ₹ 120/-

9902 F • ₹ 120/-

91 D • ₹ 120/-

8281 A • ₹ 100/-

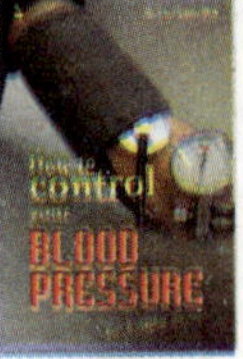

8094 D • ₹ 120/-

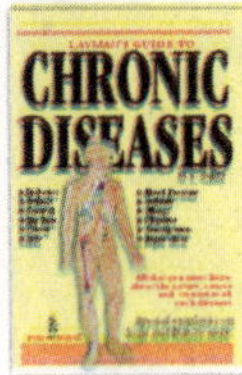

8848 D • ₹ 96/-

276 A • ₹ 96/-

8888 D • ₹ 96/-

8908 D • ₹ 120/-

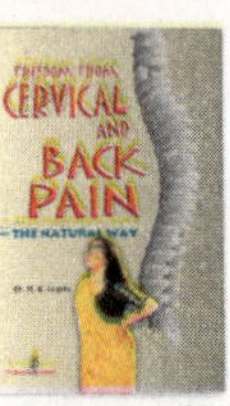

8878 B • ₹ 80/-

8277 B • ₹ 120/-

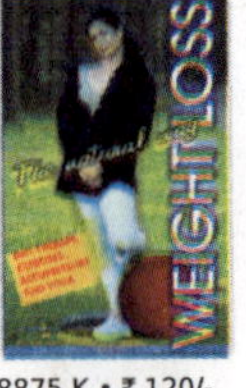

8875 K • ₹ 120/-

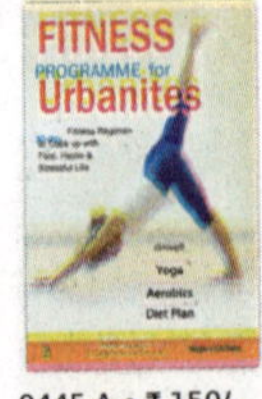

9445 A • ₹ 150/-

DIET & NUTRITION

Cooking for Diabetics

9941 D • ₹ 100/-

8904 D • ₹ 100/-

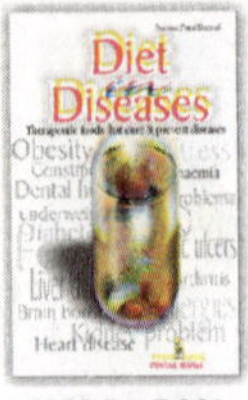

8985 B • ₹ 96/-

8968 G • ₹ 96/-

8271 C • ₹ 96/-

9037 D • ₹ 150/-